MY GIFT TO YOU

Dear Reader,

Your time is extremely valuable and you must be very discerning when deciding how to spend the holiday season. If you are looking for a resource that will help you engage with Advent in a fresh, creative, scripture-focused, and intentional way, please know that I have structured this book and its contents to the best of my ability to help you do just that.

As a thank you for purchasing this book, I am gifting you a free ebook copy of *Dwell: Advent Celebration Guide & Liturgy.*

In this companion guide, I expand on the Advent Sunday sections of this book and adapt them for a group setting, either as a family or with friends. You will find a Candle Lighting Liturgy (similar to the individual one included in this book), along with recipe and song suggestions, and discussion questions to guide your conversation over dinner.

I am a mom of three. When I can take what I am learning in my personal study and apply it in an adapted way so our whole family can learn together, I view that as a win! If you feel the same way, you will appreciate this guide.

To claim your free copy, go to dwelladventstudy.com/freeguide and use the coupon code FREEGUIDE

Enjoy and Merry Christmas!

Rachel

Audio & Video Option

To help those who better engage with content in an audio or visual format, I have created a free audio and video recording of this book.

Audio

You can find the audio version by searching "Dwell Advent Study Podcast" on any streaming podcast platform. Or visit: dwelladventstudy.com/podcast

Video

For the video recordings, you can find those by searching for my YouTube channel: Rachel Fahrenbach Books. Or visit: dwelladventstudy.com/youtube

DWELL

AN ADVENT STUDY & LITURGY

BY RACHEL FAHRENBACH

Dearborn Media

Copyright © 2023 by Rachel Fahrenbach
Published by Dearborn Mary Media
Cover and interior design by Rachel Fahrenbach

All rights reserved. No portion of this book may be reproduced, stored in a retrieval system, or transmitted in any form or by any means—electronic, mechanical, digital, photocopy, recording, or any other—except for brief quotations, without the prior permission from the publisher or author.

Unless otherwise indicated, all Scripture quotations are from the ESV® Bible (The Holy Bible, English Standard Version®), © 2001 by Crossway, a publishing ministry of Good News Publishers. Used by permission. All rights reserved.

Scripture quotations taken from the (NASB®) New American Standard Bible®, Copyright © 1960, 1971, 1977, 1995, 2020 by The Lockman Foundation. Used by permission. All rights reserved.

Scripture taken from The Voice™. Copyright © 2012 by Ecclesia Bible Society. Used by permission. All rights reserved.

Scripture quotations marked (NLT) are taken from the *Holy Bible*, New Living Translation, copyright ©1996, 2004, 2015 by Tyndale House Foundation. Used by permission of Tyndale House Publishers, Carol Stream, Illinois 60188. All rights reserved.

ISBN 978-1-7368555-2-2 (hardcover)
ISBN 978-1-7368555-7-7 (paperback)
ISBN 978-1-7368555-3-9 (ebook)

To the ones who celebrate the First Advent with me each year while anticipating the Second Advent to come...

DAD AND MOM

The ones who taught me the value of tradition, the importance of discipleship, and the overwhelmingly beautiful love of the Creator.

MY SIBLINGS

Erin, Taylor, Ceilidh, Collin, Riley, Delaney, and Addison
The ones who made the Christmases of my childhood epic, and the ones I miss dearly when distance keeps us from celebrating together.

MY HOLMES SIBLINGS-IN-LAW

Krissa, Erik, Jose, and Elena
The ones who graciously navigate the Holmes holiday frenzy year after year and have added their own unique twists to our traditions.

MY KIDS, NIECES, AND NEPHEWS

The ones who remind me to approach the holiday season (and life in general) with wonder, awe, and excitement. May you always be reminded that God desires to dwell with you.

STEVE

The one who invited me to spend every Christmas with him for the rest of my life, and I am forever grateful that he did.

A special thank you to the following writers and artists who have played a crucial supportive role in the release of this book.

BECKY BERESFORD
beckyberesford.com

Becky is an author, speaker, and coach with a Master's Certificate in Discipleship. She has a passion for helping women embrace Christ-centered empowerment through gospel truth. Her first book with Moody Publishers releases in March 2024.

SAMMY BEUKER
sammybeuker.com

Sammy tells stories to help readers grow in compassion and understanding. Her debut novel, *The Unfortunate Life of Genevieve Ryder*, released in 2023. Originally from Utah, Sammy and her family live in Michigan.

CARA BLONDO
theonethingdesired.com

Cara is passionate about helping women connect Biblical truths to their everyday lives through teaching, writing, or podcasting. Cara and her husband have been married more than 20 years and are blessed with four children.

ERICA COLAHAN
ericacolahan.com

Erica showcases God's promises of redemption and hope through short stories and historical fiction. She lives near Philadelphia with her husband and large family. Her debut novel will be published with Chrism Press in July 2024.

VICTORIA DEVINEY

Victoria creates devotionals, has a passion for the written word, and loves to share how God changes lives as they put their trust in Him. Born and raised in North Carolina, she calls the south her home despite living all over the world!

SARAH L. FRANTZ
sarahlfrantz.com

Sarah loves to weave redemptive threads through her writing, whether it's a novel, short story, or poetry. She loves to share her table in the green hills of Oklahoma where she resides with her husband and caretakes her father and his puppas.

ANGIE GIBBONS
angiegibbons.com

Angie empowers women to stress less and rediscover their joy in the family years through the *Dawn* devotional app, her writing, and Christian life coaching. Angie, her husband, and three daughters are long-time residents of Hawaii.

ERIN GRENEAUX
greneauxgardens.com

Erin creates resources for Christian moms and their kids to connect God's Word to everyday life in a way that is clear, creative, and captivating. She is an award-winning author and mom to three energetic girls.

MICHELLE HABRYCH
michellehabrych.com

Michelle helps moms through her writing and speaking. Her first book about postpartum depression, part memoir and part self-help, released in 2022. She lives in the Chicago suburbs with her family.

PAMELA HENKELMAN
pamelahenkelman.com

Pamela is a certified Empty Nest Coach, Speaker, Writer and host of *The Midlife Momma Podcast*. She has a passion to serve the often forgotten moms of adult kids. She gives them confidence in midlife and helps them flourish in their empty nests.

CASEY HILTY
caseyhilty.com

Casey is a speaker, artist, and author of *Her Children Arise*. Using storytelling and visual art, she takes mothers on a journey to fall in love with God. She and her husband, Bo, have three kids, a gaggle of pets, and call South Louisiana home.

JULIE LEFEBURE
julielefebure.com

Julie, author of *Right Now Matters* and host of the *Encouragement for Real Life Podcast*, equips women to embrace a "right now" mentality and presence so they can enjoy abundant and joy-filled lives. Living in rural Iowa, she enjoys sunrises and tandem bicycling with her husband.

AIDA MARAVILLAS
aidamaravillas.com

Aida is a writer and speaker who teaches about motherhood, mental health and parenting through a biblical lens. She helps empower moms to navigate the challenges they face. Aida lives in the Chicagoland area with her husband.

REBECCA MEEK
beccameek.com

Rebecca writes tales that tell of family, home, and leaving a legacy that matters. She has three grown children, one cool son-in-law, and an adorable mutt named Dolly. She lives with her husband in Spokane, WA.

NATALIE OGBOURNE
natalieogbourne.com

Natalie is a former Yellowstone employee and once-reluctant hiker who helps travelers plan their Yellowstone adventure and encourages them to walk by faith via tales from the trail. A lifelong Iowa resident, she has a lingering fear of cows.

AMBER JEANN PARKER
Choosejoyinthemidst.com

Amber writes on faith and mental health, primarily trauma and PTSD. She is a Physician Assistant, turned caregiver and advocate. She writes with authenticity, truth, insight, and compassion, empowering others to fight their battles from a place of strength—God's strength. She is writing her first book on mental health crisis.

KELDA LAING POYNOT
keldalaingpoynot.com

Kelda wears numerous hats: author, educator, writing coach, and homeschool consultant. She has authored six novels and three nonfiction books. She also narrates and produces her own audiobooks. She resides in South Louisiana with her husband. and labs, Darcy and Mulligan.

KATIE M. SCOTT
chasingvibrance.com

Katie is a writer and speaker who empowers women to chase vibrance in the everyday moments through practical tips, humorous stories, and Biblical encouragement. Katie is a mom of three wild and wonderful school-age children and makes her home in beautiful West Michigan with her husband.

DARA SEARCY-GARDNER
DaraSearcyGardner.com

Dara creates poetry, fiction, and music that captures the meaning and magic of life! Originally from Jos, Nigeria, Dara and her husband, two kids, and ten pets live in Portland, Oregon.

AMY SIMON
amylynnsimon.com

Amy is a Christian writer and coach. Her podcast, *The Purposeful Pen*, helps writers create a writing life that brings joy to them, glory to God, and benefit to others. She lives in Wisconsin with her husband and three kids.

KAITLIN STAFFORD
kistafford.com

Kaitlin pens fantasy stories that inspire young adults to discern truth while standing against what lurks in the dark. She pairs her passion for writing with her love of baking, creating delectable desserts that appear on both her table and within her books. Kaitlin lives in Tampa with her husband and three kids.

CYNDI STAUDT
walkingthewalkministries.com

Cyndi creates Gospel-centered content designed to make the Word easy to understand, engage with and apply. She is passionate about empowering women with Biblical truth so they can walk confidently in their purpose and live with unshakeable faith.

KATIE J TRENT
katiejtrent.com

Katie puts the fun in the FUNdamentals of family discipleship by infusing faith & food to build strong families. This homeschool mama of two has moved from the mountains to the desert, and is currently enjoying beach life.

BROOKE TURBYFILL
brooketurbyfill.com

Brooke is an author and editor who writes about spiritual practices, coaches parents about the books their kids want and need, and helps writers craft their best words. She lives in a smallish northwest corner of Georgia with two kids and a very needy, squirrely dog.

In addition to these individuals, many others have shared about this book to their friends and family. I am so very thankful for their support and cheerleading.

Contents

Introduction	1
Why Liturgy?	5
How to Use this Book	7
Advent Candle Setting & Lighting Liturgy	11
The First Advent	17
A Note about Words	19
Week One	
Week One	21
Overview	22
Advent Sunday | Dwell with God in Hope	23
Day One | Dwell on these Scriptures	27
Day Two | Dwell on these Scriptures	29
Day Three | Dwell on this Truth	31
Day Four | Dwell on these Scriptures	39
Day Five | Dwell on this Theme	41
Day Six | Dwell on this Question	45
Week Two	
Week Two	47

Overview	48
Advent Sunday | Dwell with God in Peace	49
Day One | Dwell on these Scriptures	53
Day Two | Dwell on these Scriptures	55
Day Three | Dwell on this Truth	57
Day Four | Dwell on these Scriptures	65
Day Five | Dwell on this Theme	67
Day Six | Dwell on this Question	71
Week Three	
Week Three	73
Overview	74
Advent Sunday | Dwell with God in Joy	75
Day One | Dwell on these Scriptures	79
Day Two | Dwell on these Scriptures	81
Day Three | Dwell on this Truth	83
Day Four | Dwell on these Scriptures	89
Day Five | Dwell on this Theme	91
Day Six | Dwell with this Question	95
Week Four	
Week Four	97
Overview	98
Advent Sunday | Dwell with God in Love	99
Day One | Dwell on these Scriptures	103
Day Two | Dwell on these Scriptures	105

Day Three | Dwell on this Truth	107
Day Four | Dwell on these Scriptures	113
Day Five | Dwell on this Theme	117
Day Six | Dwell on this Question	121
Christmas Day | Dwell with God in Remembrance of Immanuel	123

Week Five

Week Five	129
Overview	130
Advent Sunday | Dwell with God in Renewal	131
Day One | Dwell on these Scriptures	135
Day Two | Dwell on these Scriptures	137
Day Three | Dwell on this Truth	139
Day Four | Dwell on these Scriptures	143
Day Five | Dwell on this Theme	145
Day Six | Dwell on this Question	149

Week Six

Week Six	151
Overview	152
Advent Sunday | Dwell with God in Anticipation	153
A New Day | Dwell on this Truth	157

The Second Advent	165
Notes	167
About the Author	169

Introduction

WHEN I STARTED HAVING KIDS, I suddenly felt the need to reevaluate every family holiday tradition passed down to my husband and I—as most parents are prone to do, I suppose, when faced with the responsibility of shepherding the little soul entrusted to their care.

I enjoyed many of the fun things we did each year (you just can't beat cutting down your own Christmas tree!) but also wondered if there was a way to bring something more to this season of celebration?

I'd like to say I was diligent in exploring this question, but I pretty much put it on the back burner until I was surprised by the season's cyclical return. In my scramble to get ready for the holidays, I'd adjust a minor aspect but kept the majority of what we were doing. This pattern repeated year after year. That is, until we started practicing Sabbath.

We implemented this weekly practice[1] not out of legalism but from the understanding that there was a lot of wisdom in doing so. And, if I'm being honest, I was so burned out by the busyness of my life that if we didn't do something drastic—and quickly—I felt like I would give into the breakdown on the edge of which I was teetering.

In trying to determine what our Sabbath practice would look like each week, I learned about the idea of a Shabbat meal, a time of gathering as family and friends to celebrate God's faithful provision, feast, and rest. There is a liturgical aspect to this meal: candles are lit, blessings are uttered, songs of praise are sung, and specific food items (challah bread and wine) always grace the table. It is, as Jefferson Bethke explains in his book *To Hell with the Hustle*[2], the joy, excitement, and specialness of Christmas every week without the pressure of perfection our typical holiday season demands.

> Pausing to rest each week with God taught me that He had intentionally designed me to dwell with Him.

We were optimistic that gathering for a Shabbat meal and resting each week would be good for us. I wasn't expecting, however, how God would use this practice to shift my mindset about my identity, purpose, and belonging. Pausing to rest each week with God taught me that He had intentionally designed me to dwell with Him. And that dwelling together was to inform who I was and what I did.

Suddenly, the concept of *Immanuel* extended beyond the confines of Christmas into my every day. And, when the next holiday season rolled around, my everyday understanding of *Immanuel* deepened my understanding of its relationship to Christmas.

With this new perspective, I set out to incorporate this Sabbath posture of rest, reflection, and rejoicing into the holiday season. This book, *Dwell: An Advent Study & Liturgy*, and its companion, *Dwell: Advent Celebration Guide & Liturgy*, are my attempt to accomplish this goal.

As you approach this Advent season, I would like to encourage you to do so in light of this beautiful truth:

The God who dwelled with Adam and Eve...
The God who dwelled with Abraham, Moses, and David...
The God who dwelled with the twelve and many other disciples...
The God who dwelled with the Early Church...

...that same God desires to dwell with you.

He desires to do more than just spend time with you. He desires to live intimately with you day in and day out. He desires to partner with you in stewarding this life He has given you.

You are wanted and loved.
Redeemed and given purpose.
You are not a mistake.
You are not forgotten.

He came as the Messiah to make that known to you.
He is coming again once more to make all things right.

Come, Lord Jesus, come.

Why Liturgy?

IF YOU GREW UP IN A CHRISTIAN COMMUNITY that looked suspiciously on liturgical traditions as rote and empty, you may be skeptical about an Advent study that includes a liturgical component. I get this because I grew up in that type of church environment. It wasn't until I went away to college and experienced taking communion every single Sunday night during the campus chapel worship, that I began to see the beauty in symbolic, repeated acts of worship.

Liturgy is simply a prescribed set of repeated acts, prayers, and ceremonies that guide communal worship. It's a structured framework for believers to collectively worship and reflect together. Even if you attend a non-denominational church, that worship service has a liturgical structure to it.

But, more importantly, liturgy serves as a way to both express and shape the beliefs of the community of faith. This is why I strongly encourage you to gather weekly during this Advent season with family and/or friends to have Celebration Dinners that include this element of collective reflection and rejoicing.

I understand, however, that life can be extremely busy during the holiday season and committing to a weekly dinner to celebrate can be difficult. For those who only have the capacity for individual study, I wanted to make sure you still benefitted from the repeated act of lighting the candles each week—which is why this study contains a liturgical component for you as an individual to complete. I encourage you to still light the candles and read the accompanying scriptures out loud, even though it may feel awkward to do so by yourself. There is something impactful about tangible acts that reflect spiritual truths, especially when they engage our senses.

My hope is that as you go through this individual version this year, you will become excited about incorporating the Celebration Dinners into your observation of the Advent season next year.

Whether you chose to complete this as an individual or you chose to include Celebration Dinners, my prayer for you is that as you move through this study and liturgy, your faith will grow, your sense of identity and purpose as an image-bearer will strengthen, and your understanding of how you individually and collectively belong to God will deepen.

I also pray that this study acts as a springboard for further study. We could only cover so much in this short study! The scriptures are so rich with imagery, connections, significance, and impact; I struggled to decide what to include and what to set aside for another time. Please do not view this as the stop point about God dwelling with creation, but rather make notes as you go along to circle back to later, going deeper with your God.

Finally, enjoy this time of study! I know the words study and liturgy can feel heavy and task-driven, but they are simply tools we are using to consider the why behind the Advent celebration. When we better understand why we are celebrating, the rejoicing flows naturally.

> My prayer is that as you move through this study and liturgy, your faith will grow, your sense of identity and purpose as an image-bearer will strengthen, and your understanding of how you individually and collectively belong to God will deepen.

How to Use this Book

I STRUCTURED THIS BOOK to be completed by an individual each day during the Advent season, which typically starts four Sundays before Christmas. Each week will begin with the Candle Lighting Liturgy on Advent Sunday. During each of the remaining days of that week, you will dwell with scripture, a spiritual truth, or insightful themes regarding the Advent of Christ.

WEEKLY STRUCTURE

This study lasts for five full weeks and is meant to be **started on the first Sunday of Advent**. You will dwell on the Advent of Christ each day of the weeks leading up to Christmas and in the week to follow, **ending on the sixth Sunday** (which will land somewhere near the Day of Epiphany).

Each week has a themed focus:
Week 1: God Dwells with Us in the Garden
Week 2: God Dwells with Us in the Desert
Week 3: God Dwells with Us in Jerusalem
Week 4: God Dwells with Us in the Messiah
Week 5: God Dwells with Us in Us
Week 6: God Dwells with Us in the New Creation

The Advent Sunday sections within this book are designed for individual liturgy. As I mentioned before, my heart is that individuals will study on their own during the week and gather together with others on the Advent Sundays to light the candles, eat together, reflect on scriptural truth (possibly discussing insights from their personal study), and rejoice over God's goodness and faithfulness. If you will be gathering with others on Advent Sunday, you will want to use the companion guide.

If your Sabbath practice lands on another day of the week other than Sunday, the Candle Lighting Liturgy within the Advent Sunday section of each week can easily be adjusted to that day. You will need to start during the week before the traditional advent start that year to make it work.

For example: at the time of this book's release it is 2023. This year, Advent starts on Sunday, December 3rd. But, my family gathers for a Shabbat meal on Friday nights not Sunday. So, I could complete the sections in this book marked Advent Sunday on Fridays, starting December 1st, the Friday before Advent traditionally begins.

If your experience of the holidays in past years has been one of a whirlwind, I would like to invite you to consider actually **scheduling time on your calendar each day** for this study and the Candle Lighting Liturgy (or the Celebration Dinners if you do them). Don't treat it like a to-do! Instead, treat it like an event to show up to, ready and excited.

DAILY STRUCTURE

If the idea of needing to carve out time each day in this busy season worries you, let me take a moment to assure you. I am a busy mom myself, so I tried to design each day to be completed in about **30 minutes each day**. However, how long it takes you to complete that day's task will depend on how quickly you move through the content.

I have also intentionally **varied the type of content** you will engage with each day to keep things interesting. While I hate to admit it, and even though I value structure and repetition, my creative brain can get bored easily with the same thing day in and day out. If you too struggle with this, I see you and tried to craft this study in a way to help with that challenge. The daily structure is as follows:

Advent Sunday | Dwell with God
Light candle(s) and spend time in reflection and rejoicing.

Days 1, 2 & 4 | Dwell on these Scriptures
Read and meditate on God's word.

Day 3: Dwell on this Truth
Read a fictionalized story of scriptural truth.

Day 5: Dwell on this Theme
Further dig into the overarching theme for this week.

Day 6: Dwell on This Question
Contemplate how this week's theme impacts your personal life.

While you will want to **systematically complete each day** as they build on each other, some days will require more time than others and you may need to jump around to accommodate your schedule.

Because each day varies, I created an **Overview page** at the beginning of each week's section. This serves as a table of contents and guide for the week.

PREPARATION

I tried to keep things as simple for you as possible to incorporate this study and liturgy into your Advent observation. Before the start of the Advent season, you will need to do a few things to prep:

1. Identify the first Sunday of Advent for the current year (this will be your start day for the study).

2. Gather and assemble your Advent Candle Setting (more on this in the next section).

3. Gather or make the Ornaments or Labels (if using; more on this in the next section).

4. Select a notebook to use for the journaling prompts on Day Six. You can also use it make observations, take notes, mark down things you wish to study further, and journal out prayers.

If you are including the weekly Celebration Dinners, you will need to give yourself some time to prepare for those dinners (I have found the Thursday before a good day to assess and prepare). The *Celebration Guide* has all the information you will need to prepare and implement these dinners.

In the next section, I'll go over what you need for your Candle Setting.

Advent Candle Setting & Lighting Liturgy

THE ADVENT SEASON HAS BEEN TRADITIONALLY MARKED by the church with a series of candle lightings on the four Sundays before Christmas day. At the beginning of each week of this study, you will do the same. You might be wondering why light candles at all? Why not do something else?

This candle lighting practice reminds us of a few things:

- The creation story (darkness covered the deep and God said "Let there be light")

- The story of Jesus (Jesus is the "light of the world" and a literal light, the Bethlehem star, shone over his birthplace)

- The purpose of the Church (we are to be a light to the world)

- The renewal of creation (God's reigning presence will be our source of light in the New Creation)

There isn't anything particularly special or sacred about candles but, when lit, they create an environment that welcomes the special and the sacred. We use them on birthday cakes, to elevate anniversary dinners, or even to release a calming scent into the room. In the writing community, many authors use the lighting of a candle to signal it's time to start creating. For the Advent season, candles help us mark this time as a special anniversary and, when used in a liturgical practice, remind us of significant and impactful Biblical truths.

CANDLE SETTING ASSEMBLY

Sometime before the first Sunday of Advent (or your first adjusted start day), you will need to assemble your Advent Candle Setting.

ITEMS NEEDED
7 White Candles (1 should be a bit taller than the others)
Evergreen Branches
Tray for Candles
Lighter or Matches

For Advent, you may have seen the use of an evergreen wreath (representing God's eternal nature), three purple candles (representing royalty), one pink candle (representing joy), and a white candle in the center to represent Christ. The wreath may have included berries (representing Christ's blood) and pinecones (representing Christ's resurrection).

For this study, however, **we will set up the candles differently** and add a few more. I know this might be odd for you if you have grown up with the traditional Advent wreath in your home or church, but I hope you'll allow for the adjustments and, as you move through the study, will see why I've made them.

Instead of setting our candles within a wreath, **we will line up our candles in a row**. We will still include evergreen branches, but will weave them in and out of the candles. This signifies that the story of creation had a specific beginning and was meant to dwell in God's presence eternally. But, sinful disobedience broke the original design, setting creation into a linear trajectory of redemption. Creation's story has moved forward in time, first towards the Advent of Christ in Bethlehem and now towards the Second Advent of Christ that will make all things new.

Instead of four candles, **we will use seven white candles**, with one being a slightly taller candle (this will be our Christ candle). I personally prefer pillar candles as they are more sturdy, but you can use whatever you wish. We will situate the **CHRIST CANDLE in the**

middle with three of the smaller candles to the left and right of it. They are all white to remind us of God's enduring, merciful character of forgiveness towards us. **Each of the six candles sits on a tray** (you can use whatever you want) to represent the heaven-meets-earth spaces (you might even call them temples) God has dwelled with humanity.

LIGHTING LITURGY

If you are familiar with the Advent wreath, you'll notice throughout this study that I have incorporated the traditional names for the candles, but expanded on their symbolism in light of the bigger theme of God dwelling with humanity that we are exploring this Advent season.

Week One
God Dwells with Us: In the Garden
Candle Label: Hope/Prophecy
Expanded Theme: Promised Hope

Week Two
God Dwells with Us: In the Tabernacle
Candle Label: Peace/Bethlehem
Expanded Theme: Redeemed Peace

Week Three
God Dwells with Us: In Jerusalem
Candle Label: Joy/Shepherd
Expanded Theme: Deeply-rooted Joy

Week Four
God Dwells with Us: In the Messiah
Candle Label: Love/Angel
Expanded Theme: Sacrificial Love

Week Five (Not Traditionally Included)
God Dwells with Us: In Us

Candle Label: Renewal/Church
Expanded Theme: Ongoing Renewal

Week Six (Not Traditionally Included)
God Dwells with Us: In the New Creation
Candle Label: Anticipation/Celebration
Expanded Theme: Second Advent

We will light the CHRIST CANDLE each Sunday as we read from John 1:1-3 in addition to lighting the specific candle(s) for that week. This signifies that while He was born as a baby in Bethlehem, Jesus has and always will be God. He is the Alpha and the Omega, the Beginning and the End, the First and the Last.

As the weeks progress, we will continue to light the candles from the previous weeks. This growing light signifies that we are progressively getting closer to the final return of Christ, which will drive out all darkness (Rev 21:4).

ORNAMENTS AND CANDLE LABELS (OPTIONAL)

Within the liturgy for each Advent Sunday, you will see an option to hang an ornament on the tree or add a label to your candle. This is completely optional but it is a fun way to involve and engage the kids at your table.

For candle labels, I suggest checking Pinterest for numerous DIY ideas. Amazon or Esty may have done-for-you options as well.

Our family uses ornaments and hangs them on our Christmas tree when we light the corresponding candle. You are welcome to use whatever feels significant to you, but here is what we have used for reference:

- Weeks 1-4: Ornaments with the words Hope, Peace, Joy, and Love.

- Christmas Day: An ornament that portrays the nativity scene.

- Week 5: A church ornament to represent the renewal that happens in and through the lives of believers.

- Week 6: An ornament with the Greek letters Alpha & Omega as a reference to the Second Advent (coming) of Christ.

Whatever you choose to do, the main purpose is to bring a visual reminder into your space of the themes we are exploring during the Advent season. Get as creative as you'd like and have fun with it!

The First Advent

LUKE 4:16-21 And [Jesus] came to Nazareth, where he had been brought up. And as was his custom, he went to the synagogue on the Sabbath day, and he stood up to read. And the scroll of the prophet Isaiah was given to him. He unrolled the scroll and found the place where it was written:

> "The Spirit of the Lord is upon me, because he has anointed me to proclaim good news to the poor. He has sent me to proclaim liberty to the captives and recovering of sight to the blind, to set at liberty those who are oppressed, to proclaim the year of the Lord's favor."[3]

And he rolled up the scroll and gave it back to the attendant and sat down. And the eyes of all in the synagogue were fixed on him. And he began to say to them, "Today this Scripture has been fulfilled in your hearing."

A Note about Words

THE FOLLOWING WORDS will be used often as we consider what it means for God to be *with us*. Below, I have compiled some common definitions of these words.[4]

Dwell (verb)

1. to stay in one place for a period of time

2. to take up residence in a place

3. to place focus or attention

Tabernacle (noun)

1. a place dedicated to worship

2. an object used to house the consecrated elements of the Eucharist

3. the sanctuary tent referenced in the Bible

4. a shelter, temporary or permanent (not typically used in modern language)

Tabernacle (intransitive verb):

tabernacled; tabernacling

    1. to temporarily reside

    2. to indwell a physical body

Note: An intransitive verb doesn't need an object immediately following it. If there is a word following it, that word won't answer *what?* or *whom?*. Instead, it'll answer questions like *where?*, *when?*, *how?*, or *for how long?*.

Temple (noun)

    1. a building dedicated to worship

    2. a dedicated space for a specific purpose

Advent (noun)

    1. a timeframe starting four Sundays prior to Christmas, observed by Christians in remembrance of Christ's birth

    2. the coming of Christ as described in the Gospels

    3. the second coming of Christ

    4. the arrival of a person, thing, or state of being

WEEK ONE
GOD DWELLS WITH US
IN THE GARDEN

Week One | Overview

ADVENT SUNDAY/SABBATH

Dwell with God: In Hope

DAY ONE

Dwell on these Scriptures: Genesis 1

DAY TWO

Dwell on these Scriptures: Genesis 2; Exodus 20:11

DAY THREE

Dwell on this Truth: God's enduring desire is to dwell with us, to co-rule with us, and to co-create with us. When humanity makes a mess of things, God's enduring promise is one of hopeful reconciliation and restoration.

DAY FOUR

Dwell on these Scriptures: Genesis 3

DAY FIVE

Dwell on this Theme: Promised Hope—Because God is faithful to keep His promises, we hope. (Heb 10:23)

DAY SIX

Dwell on this Question: Do I take God at His word, expecting Him to keep His promises?

Advent Sunday I Dwell with God in Hope

PREPARE

Candle Set & Lighter
HOPE Ornament or Candle Label (if using)
Bible

Set aside distractions during this time of worship, reflection, and remembrance. Today, focus your thoughts on God's faithfulness in keeping His promises and the hope we have because of it.

As you light the CHRIST CANDLE, read John 1:1-3 out loud:

> In the beginning was the Word, and the Word was with God, and the Word was God. He was in the beginning with God. All things were made through him, and without Him was not anything made that was made.

REFLECT

In a moment, you will light the HOPE CANDLE (also sometimes called the Prophecy Candle). As you do, reflect on the following:

In the Beginning God created a cosmic dwelling place, the heavens and the earth, a tabernacle where He and His creation could reside together. He desired to share His authority and so He made humanity, the male Adam and the female Eve, in His image and gave them purpose: co-rule, co-steward, and co-create, both with Him and with each other.

But soon, Adam and Eve chose to doubt God's good provision as enough and took what was not given to them. In doing so, they rebelled against God, sinned, and damaged their home and their relationship with God. No longer could they reside with God in that cosmic dwelling place, so they had to leave. But, before they left their dwelling space with God, He gave a promise of hope: one day, a conqueror would make things right.

We light the CANDLE OF HOPE to remember the prophecies of hope given throughout scripture that pointed to the coming Messiah. We remember how the Israelites waited in hopeful expectation and anticipation, believing God would be faithful in His promise to send a redeemer.

Please light the HOPE CANDLE.

We read scripture to be reminded of God's truth. In Psalms 33, we read the truth that God is trustworthy and faithful. We can put our hope in Him. Read the following portion of Psalms 33:

> Shout for joy in the Lord, O you righteous! Praise befits the upright. Give thanks to the Lord with the lyre; make melody to him with the harp of ten strings! Sing to him a new song; play skillfully on the strings, with loud shouts. For the word of the Lord is upright, and all his work is done in faithfulness. He loves righteousness and justice; the

earth is full of the steadfast love of the Lord.

By the word of the Lord the heavens were made, and by the breath of his mouth all their host. He gathers the waters of the sea as a heap; he puts the deeps in storehouses. Let all the earth fear the Lord; let all the inhabitants of the world stand in awe of him! For he spoke, and it came to be; he commanded, and it stood firm. The Lord brings the counsel of the nations to nothing; he frustrates the plans of the peoples. The counsel of the Lord stands forever, the plans of his heart to all generations.

Blessed is the nation whose God is the Lord, the people whom he has chosen as his heritage!...Our soul waits for the Lord; he is our help and our shield. For our heart is glad in him, because we trust in his holy name. Let your steadfast love, O Lord, be upon us, even as we hope in you.

REJOICE

If you have a HOPE ornament or a candle label, you may add it to your tree or candle at this time. When you see it there, may it remind you that the hope we have in God is a gift from Him. A reminder that He loves us and desires to dwell with us.

Take a moment to give thanks:

> Father God, thank You for Your desire to dwell with humanity. Thank You for having compassion, mercy, and grace on humanity, even when we rebelled against You. Throughout this week, may I remember that I can HOPE in You because You are faithful to keep your promises. Amen.

Throughout this Advent season, you will be introduced to generations who cried out "Come, our Lord, come!" while waiting for the Messiah. Today, we remember that Jesus is that Messiah and that He will one day return to redeem and make right the world. As you close this time of reflection and rejoicing, add your voice with those generations before and pray:

Come, Lord Jesus, come.

Day One | Dwell on these Scriptures

READ GENESIS 1 through one time.

Reread the passage with the following in mind:

If you have grown up in church, you may be tempted to read through these verses at a quick pace. It will feel familiar and simple. God spoke and it was good, right?

But, today, as you read through this chapter, imagine it is a letter addressed to you. In it, the author details the intentional arrangements He's made for your time together. Every action listed underscores the careful anticipation of your needs.

As you read, consider how He prepares the structure of limits, first with time and then with the environment. Remember, God is infinite, existing outside the boundaries of time and space. But, we are finite. In order to dwell with us, He establishes a cosmic tabernacle.

As you read, consider how He anticipates your physical needs. The complex system of the environment sustains the complex system of your body. From the oxygen you breathe to the plants you eat to the way the moon triggers re-energizing sleep, every aspect matters.

As you read, consider how you are created in the image of a creative God, which means you are inherently creative. Consider what creativity looks like in Genesis 1. How would you define creativity after reading this chapter?

As you read, consider which part of creation (the ground, the sky, the sea, the animals, etc.) most deeply connects with your soul. Your creator put that part of creation here for you to enjoy. Take a moment to thank Him.

Day Two | Dwell on these Scriptures

READ GENESIS 2:1-24 AND EXODUS 20:1 through one time.

Reread the passages with the following in mind:

There are two different Hebrew words that get translated into the English word "rest"[5]:

1. *shabat* - to cease from

2. *nuakh* - to take up residence (in a safe, secure, and stable space)

In English, this nuance is missed but it provides an important distinction. God both ceases from His preparations because they were complete (Genesis 2:2) and then takes up residence (dwells) with His creation within His creation (Exodus 20:11).[6]

In fact, in Genesis 2:15, this word *nuakh* appears again when God places Adam into the garden to work and keep it. Some translations will say "God rested Adam" while others will say "God put Adam" but we can also read it as "God resided Adam" in Eden. In other words, Adam dwelled (lived in a particular way, was at home, and fully present) in the garden.

As you read these verses, consider how God doesn't plant the garden until He has created humanity to cultivate and steward it.

As you read these verses, consider how God intentionally created His cosmic tabernacle so both He and humanity could dwell together, co-creating, co-working and co-ruling.

As you read, consider the implication these verses have on both humanity's identity and purpose. What implications does it have on your personal sense of identity and purpose?

Day Three | Dwell on this Truth

God's enduring desire is to dwell with us, to co-rule with us and to co-create with us. When humanity makes a mess of things, God's enduring promise is one of hopeful reconciliation and restoration.

IMAGE-BEARER: EVE

The question is posed to me.

"What is this that you've done?"

And in me.

"What is this that you've done?"

And through me.

"What is this that you've done?"

And around me.

"What is this that you've done?"

He is the very breath that I take in as I search for words to form my answer. Though there is no room for explanation, only admission, because He is known and He knows.

And yet, knowing this, just moments before, I stood at the base of the tree and convinced myself to push away what was known for a promise of what was not.

For the first time since my first breath, vines have taken up residence inside my mind and strangle the light from my thoughts, dimming truth and understanding.

I roll the thick stem of a fig leaf pinched between my thumb and finger as if the subtle vibration will knock the vines loose. I reverse the movement and the leaf twirls in the opposite direction.

A question found me at the base of the tree, a question dipped in an opportunity to know what was unknown: an existence without Him.

Without Him in me.
And through me.
And around me.

An existence where He is not known and I am not known.
An existence without His presence ever-dwelling with creation.
An existence without His oversight: solo-ruling humanity.

Within the promise of insight, I forgot the promise of purpose: Image-bearer. Male and female He created us to reflect Him in the task of stewardship, co-rulers within the space of His cosmic tabernacle.

I forgot and reached up.
I forgot and took hold.
I forgot.

"The serpent's deception caused me to forget," a whisper of admission pushes past the lump of shame and guilt in my throat, "and I ate."

He knows.
And I am known.

And in that space of the known, I am aware of the edges of what once was unknown—an existence without Him—swallowing the corners of the garden as it inches forward, extinguishing the light that emanates deep from within creation...

...and through creation...
...and around creation...

...leaving a dullness where once there was vibrance.

This new known, a slow snuffing out of divine presences, triggers something new within my chest.

Fear.
Fear of death.

And this fear is greater than my fear of His judgment.

My eyes snap from the ground to His face and focus with panic.
He meets my gaze with the unexpected: forgiveness.

We will not die.

But, just as I am certain we will not die, I am also certain we will not live either. At least, not live in the way we have known living to be.

I glance sideways at Adam. He hasn't noticed how the edge touches the color of creation and dims the radiance. He is focused on the pronounced judgment over the serpent. With the finality that accompanies those words, he glances my way and I see he thinks we are in the clear, that we will be okay. His optimism fades, though, as he sees the life-disrupting edges consuming the ground just beyond me.

He swallows hard. Panic replaces assurance.

Beyond Adam, I notice the edge inches its way up the trunk of the fig tree and consumes each leaf. Earlier, we created covers of protection from those very leaves. How did we not know there is no protection from the consequence of treason?

I thought knowing would be slow and illuminating like the rising sun, but, I now know it is the slow setting sun that leaves the world visionless.

As the dimness takes the light out from the very last leaf on the longest branch of the tree, His words command my attention and I will myself to take my eyes off that edge of dimness and focus on His face.

His pronouncement layers pain and suffering into my image-bearer role. The words feel other-wordly and the situation incomprehensible. I know this is important, that it will have a long-lasting impact, but the dimness closing in poses the imminent threat.

He turns to Adam and tells of the struggle that will be between him and the ground. Adam stands silently after the pronouncement is finished, letting the truth settle over him. He glances to the edge of dimness that has picked up speed and is swallowing whole plants at a time before bringing his gaze back to me. There is an acceptance shrouding his countenance as he simply says, "You will be called Eve."

My spirit meets the renaming as presumption and I feel the friction deeply. The name removes my oneness with Adam and establishes my identity squarely in what I can produce. It feels like both a compliment bestowed and a wall of division erected. I reach out and grab his hand to stabilize the conflict within me but drop it when the usual electric current of connection is not there.

It is then that I see the animal skins fashioned into coverings for Adam and I lying on the ground at our feet. My stomach drops as I see the deep brown and white fur and immediately recognize the animal that once wore it. Blood has been shed to provide covering. The brutality of it, and the necessity of it, feels like another source of friction.

He first clothes Adam and then He turns His attention to me. Gently, tenderly, He wraps me with the covering, holding me at arms length to assess His workmanship. He makes no statement but I can see that He is satisfied.

Fear prickles my spine up into the base of my skull as the vines unwrap from my mind and the light of clarity regains its footing: we can no longer know Him. At least, not the way we have, not in His dwelling place. We seized insight into what we didn't know and that act has cost us what we did know: intimacy breathing life into the very skin of our being.

I will no longer be one with Adam.
And I will no longer dwell with Adonai.

The finality of that statement reaches into the depths of my innermost being and draws out lament. I drop to my knees and fall forward on my hands. Another wail escapes as I see the garden is nearly completely eaten by the dimness. Adam's arms wrap around my shoulders, trying to both comfort me and raise me from the ground but I fight him with a newfound strength fueled by anger, anxiety, and distress. That is, until I see the edge of dimness just feet away from my fingertips.

The weight of my sudden retreat from the edge throws Adam off-balance and he tumbles into the dirt next to me. I crawl away from the edge and towards Adonai, rising to my feet halfway and covering the remaining distance in a run. When I reach Him, I throw myself down at His feet, ignoring the pain as my knees hit the ground, and sob "Please! No!"

Even as the words abscond my lips, I know they are futile but I repeat the word "please" with desperation tinging my voice. "Please, don't turn me away from you." My body convulses with the weight of exile and I close my eyes against the reality of my next statement: "If I cannot live with You, I will die apart from You."

The air has become heavier and my lungs burn as I take in breaths quicker than I am used to. The sounds too, have become different, distorted. The light-amplified color is not the only thing the edge has taken.

The electric current of connection from His hand on the side of my head startles me but I respond with a shake of refusal, closing my eyes even tighter. I am terrified of what will greet me if I open them. But,

He doesn't ask me to. Instead, He whispers into my ear what He spoke over the serpent:

"I'm declaring war between you and the woman. Between your offspring and hers. He'll wound your head, you'll wound his heel."

And with that declaration follows a vision of a being who carries both the image of Adonai and His very essence. The Redeemer, the one will restore and make right the world. The one who will push back the edge and make a way to once again dwell in His presence. To once again know as well as be known.

My eyes fly open and I gasp for breath, reaching out to cling to Him but my hands meet nothing and I fall forward, the gravel piercing the softness of my palms once again. As a stabilizing peace covers me, I am aware of the permission to feel deeply the grief that has taken up residence within my soul.

He breathes His special name for me, the one that belongs only to Him, over my being and a strength spreads from the top of my head to the tips of my fingers and toes. I rise from the ground and stand before Him.

I stand before Him known.
But even more than that, I stand before Him loved.

His wanted creation.

He takes my hand and places it in Adam's as the last crevices of the garden are consumed by the edge of dimness. We keep our eyes on Him until all has been consumed and we can no longer see Him.

It is done.
We have been sent out.

I drop Adam's hand and take a step forward. I cannot see it but I know the Garden is still there. A low growl meets my ears first and then the sight of cherubim with their swords of fire meet my eyes.

I step back out of respect for the spiritual beings, but then I stand still, searching for Him. He is still there, still able to be known, but it feels different. Like how I know Adam's arm is still under the animal skin, and how I can feel the form of it, but I cannot touch His skin, cannot feel the heat emanating from it. I can still know Adonai on this side of the separation but it will not be the same. At least, not until...

I turn to Adam. "He will come, The Redeemer."

Adam nods. "Yes."

"And all will be made right."

He nods again. "Yes."

"And Adonai will dwell with us once more."

Adam sighs, relief settling into his being as he contemplates my words. "Yes." He holds out his hand. "It's time for us to go," he says with resolve.

I place my hand into his and together we venture into what once was unknown.

Day Four | Dwell on these Scriptures

READ GENESIS 3 through one time.

Reread the passage with the following in mind:

This is another familiar passage of scripture for many of us who grew up in the Church. It can be hard to read it without imagining the illustrated scene from whatever children's Bible you grew up reading (it popped into your mind just now didn't it?).

Unfortunately, we grew up with this one-dimensional image of Adam and Eve instead of the flesh and blood reality that both initiated Heaven on Earth (and humanity's role within it) and, successively, fractured it into devastating separation. This one short story establishes the ongoing tension within the soul of every individual between wanting to be reunited with the Creator as a co-ruler and wanting to become the ruling creator themselves.

As you read these scriptures, consider how this tension is teased into being by the crafty serpent casting doubt and suspicion. Consider how Eve took the serpent at his word instead of taking her very own faithful, kind, and loving Creator at His word. How often have you done the same?

As you read, consider the symbolism of Adam and Eve choosing the fig leaf for a cover. Fig trees are often planted in a vineyard to provide protection for grapes from the harsh elements. Contrast this with the cover of skins given later by God. Consider how even with their new-found knowledge, humanity still didn't fully understand what was required to dwell within the presence of God.

As you read, consider how God dialogues with Adam and Eve, never pronouncing shame but announcing consequences, holding each accountable for their part in the choice to rebel.

As you read, consider the mercy God extends by turning Adam and Eve out of the garden. If they ate of the Tree of Life and gained the ability to live forever, they would live forever in a fallen state of separation. By exiling them, God set into motion His plan for restoring humanity's ability to dwell with Him.

Day Five | Dwell on this Theme

Promised Hope
We hope because God is faithful to keep His promises.

> I will put enmity between you and the woman, and between your offspring and her offspring; he shall bruise your head and you shall bruise his heel. Genesis 3:15

In scripture, hope is treated as a verb, not a noun, unlike what we do with it in our westernized English. Hope, for us, is a state of wishful thinking. We have a desired outcome and we wish for it to come true. We don't have an assurance one way or another. We want it to happen, but there is no guarantee that what we want will come to pass.

But, for the Biblical authors, hope was synonymous with expectation, anticipation, and trust. How interesting, then, that trust is the very thing Eve had a problem with at the foot of the tree. When faced with a choice to hope in the Creator with whom she dwelled, she chose doubt.

Hebrews 10:23 is a perfect example of how the word hope is used by the early church: "Let us hold fast the confession of our hope without wavering, for he who promised is faithful."

While the sentiment within this statement is strong on its own, when read within the context of the passage, it becomes a testament to

God's desire to dwell with us and His execution of the restorative plan to do so. Within chapter 10 of Hebrews, we read of how God gave the Israelites a way to dwell with Him (we'll read more about this during the next two weeks), but how God's ultimate desire was to reconcile with His creation so that He could dwell and co-rule not just with Israel, but with humanity as a whole.

Israel waited in hope for the promises of God to materialize. They didn't wish God would keep His word, they KNEW and EXPECTED God to keep His promises. Later, when the Messiah died, rose, and ascended into Heaven, the early church waited with hope that one day He would return because He had promised to do so.

The author of Hebrews reminds us that we hold fast our confession that we are forgiven and given access to God through the shed blood of Christ. The flimsy fig-covering of our own construct won't cut it, we need the covering of His design. It is the perfect covering, the one that was promised all the way back in Genesis chapter three.

Israel's confession was that of expected hope for a messiah. The early church's confession was that of expected hope for full forgiveness and the indwelling of the Holy Spirit.

Do we hold fast our confession of hope? Do we take God at His word that Christ's sacrifice was the promised restorative plan? Do we trust that because of Christ's death and resurrection, we have been restored to co-dweller and co-ruler status?

Do we wait with expectation and anticipation? Do we hope for:

1. God to use us to tell others about the redemption offered through Christ and to bring the world back into communion with Him?

2. The full restoration of Heaven on earth with the return of Christ?

This far removed from the early church, we have lost the sense of urgency and nearness of the return of Christ. Add to that, the dissenting and confusing views of eschatology (the study of end-times), and we have become a group of believers worried more about the present than about a future we don't expect to see in our lifetime. But, we have this hope, God is faithful to forgive, faithful to redeem, and faithful to restore. He has promised to return and right all things into propriety.

In this present day, let's move with hope for the future because God is faithful to keep His promises.

Day Six | Dwell on this Question

Do I take God at His word, expecting Him to keep His promises?

JOURNAL YOUR RESPONSES to the questions below:

Do I take God at His word, expecting Him to keep His promises for forgiveness, redemption, and restoration?

Do I live each day with expectation, anticipation, *hope*? Or do I live in a state of wishful thinking?

Do I believe God's promises are for my present and my future, or do I attribute them to some distant past?

What promise of God do I struggle with doubting?

Take a moment to write out your personal confession of hope.

WEEK TWO
GOD DWELLS WITH US
IN THE TABERNACLE

Week Two | Overview

ADVENT SUNDAY/SABBATH

Dwell with God: In Peace

DAY ONE

Dwell on these Scriptures: Exodus 15:1-21

DAY TWO

Dwell on these Scriptures: Exodus 20:1-21; Deuteronomy 5

DAY THREE

Dwell on this Truth: God desired to dwell with Israel and make them a priestly model of His garden-kingdom where humans co-rule and co-create with Him. Once again, humanity falls short and once again God is faithful to forgive. When Israel responds by obediently following His commands, they experience *shalom*.

DAY FOUR

Dwell on these Scriptures: Exodus 34:1-10; Exodus 20:8-11; Deuteronomy 5:12-15; Exodus 25:1-9

DAY FIVE

Dwell on this Theme: Redeemed Peace—God's redemptive plan prioritizes our complete well-being, our peace. (Col 1:19-20)

DAY SIX

Dwell on this Question: Do I truly believe that the redemptive work of Jesus' death and resurrection has brought *shalom* to my life?

Advent Sunday I Dwell with God in Peace

PREPARE

Candle Set & Lighter
PEACE Ornament or Candle Label (if using)
Bible

Set aside distractions during this time of worship, reflection, and remembrance. Focus your thoughts on the redemption God extended to us and the peace that is a result.

As you light the CHRIST CANDLE, read John 1:1-3 out loud:

> In the beginning was the Word, and the Word was with God, and the Word was God. He was in the beginning with God. All things were made through him, and without Him was not anything made that was made.

REFLECT

Light the HOPE CANDLE and remember how God has faithfully fulfilled His promises. Soon you will light the PEACE CANDLE (also sometimes called the Bethlehem Candle). As you do reflect on the following:

In the Generations that followed Adam and Eve, God chose various individuals to be part of His plan for redemption. He established the nation of Israel through Abraham, Isaac, and Jacob, promising to send the Messiah through their bloodline. Eventually, this family left their home for Egypt and, over the span of hundreds of years, became slaves and oppressed within that city. But, God had chosen Israel to be His people and to make His dwelling among them for His future purpose of creating *shalom*, peace, between Himself and His creation.

Using both the leadership of Moses and miraculous events, God delivered Israel from Egypt's oppression in order to dwell with them. The events of the Passover and exodus serve as a physical reminder of a spiritual truth: since the rebellious choice of Adam and Eve, we are all held captive by sin, unable to free ourselves. But, God's redemptive plan includes both deliverance and a renewed dwelling with Him.

We light the PEACE CANDLE as a reminder that God did more than just deliver Israel from Egypt. He invited them to dwell with Him and follow His commands, restoring their role in blessing the nations as His representatives. He offered them *shalom*, peace, in their present as they waited for the ultimate *shalom*-bringer, Jesus, who would be born in Bethlehem.

Please light the PEACE CANDLE.

We read scripture to be reminded of God's truth. In Isaiah 26, we read about the peace God extends to us when we put our trust in Him. Read this portion of Isaiah:

> In that day this song will be sung in the land of Judah: "We have a strong city; he sets up salvation as walls and bulwarks. Open the gates, that the righteous nation that keeps faith may enter in. You keep him in perfect peace whose mind is stayed on you, because he trusts in you.

> Trust in the Lord forever, for the Lord God is an everlasting rock. For he has humbled the inhabitants of the height, the lofty city. He lays it low, lays it low to the ground, casts it to the dust... O Lord, we wait for you; your name and remembrance are the desire of our soul. My soul yearns for you in the night; my spirit within me earnestly seeks you... O Lord, your hand is lifted up, but they do not see it... O Lord, you will ordain peace for us, for you have indeed done for us all our works. Isaiah 26:1-12

REJOICE

If you have a PEACE ornament or candle label, you can add it to your tree or candle at this time. As you see it there, may it remind you that the peace we have through God's redemption is a gift from Him. A reminder that He loves us and desires to dwell with us.

Take a moment to give thanks:

> Father God, thank You for Your desire to dwell with us. Thank You for both your desire for peace between You and Your creation and your redemptive plan to make it happen. Throughout this week may I remember that I can dwell with You in PEACE because You have delivered us from our captivity to sin and redeemed us. Amen.

Throughout this Advent season, we will be introduced to generations who cried out "Come, our Lord, come!" while waiting for the Messiah. Today, we remember that Jesus is that Messiah and that He will one day return to redeem and make right the world. As you close this time of reflection and rejoicing, add your voice with those generations before and pray:

Come, Lord Jesus, come.

Day One | Dwell on these Scriptures

READ EXODUS 15:1-21 through one time.

Reread the passage with the following in mind:

It is tempting to think the exodus story is all about getting Israel out of Egypt and to the Promised Land, but freeing His people was simply Act I. The full plan unfolds in the second half of the book. This song of documentation and praise is the intermission before Act II.

As you read, consider how within ancient Egyptian religious and political beliefs, the pharaoh was considered divine, an earthly manifestation of the gods tasked with ruling. Israel was enslaved within this context and by this man.

Note how the battle between God and the pharaoh is decidedly one-sided, with God easily defeating him. No one, not pharaoh or any other gods, compares to the awe-inspiring magnificence and unparalleled nature of God's holiness and steadfast love.

Consider as you read how Israel casts off their identity as slaves belonging to Pharaoh and asserts their belonging to Yahweh, the God of their forefathers. By acknowledging this history, they reclaim their identity as Israel and remember God's covenant with Abraham, Isaac, and Jacob.

As you read these verses, consider how this song both summarizes what has happened and casts a vision for what is to come.

Note the way verse 17 mirrors the imagery of Genesis chapter two where God "plants" Adam in Eden to work it. While the mountain mentioned here most likely refers to Mt. Zion in Jerusalem, consider how God intends to dwell with Israel in the interim. In a full-circle moment, He brings them back to the sacred space where He met Moses to discuss their deliverance. Now, He brings Israel there to discuss what it means to dwell with Him and work in this sacred dwelling place.

Day Two | Dwell on these Scriptures

READ EXODUS 20:1-21 AND DEUTERONOMY 5 through one time.

Reread these passages with the following in mind:

The Ten Commandments are pretty well covered in Children's Church. Keeping it simple for little minds, these commands are often taught as a list of to-dos to be memorized. Unfortunately, we bring this mindset into adulthood, treating this list as a way to be moral instead of a contract between God and Israel, the terms and conditions for establishing Israel as a beacon of hope and peace in the darkness of the world.

As you read these two passages, note how they vary slightly. It is important to understand that they are written in two different contexts for two different purposes: one (Exodus) to document the historic act of deliverance and covenant-making, and the other (Deuteronomy) to review, instruct, and encourage a new generation regarding the covenant before they enter the Promised Land.

As you read, consider how Moses speaks to Israel in Deuteronomy as if they were there at Mt. Sinai when the Ten Commandments were first issued. Why do you think he does this? How does this correlate to the statement of God's character in Exodus 20:5-6 and Deuteronomy 5:9-10?

Consider how God identifies Himself as redeemer before issuing the commands. This is not an arbitrary list of morals but what is to be true because of God's character as the supreme authority of creation.

As you read the two accounts of what happened after the commandments were given, consider how the Israelites had a healthy fear of the power of God's presence (although they missed out on the merciful invitation to draw near) and how God ties this level of respect to the abundant life that flows from following His commands.

Day Three | Dwell on this Truth

God desired to dwell with Israel and make them a priestly model of His Garden-Kingdom where humans co-rule and co-create with Him. Once again, humanity falls short and once again God is faithful to forgive. When Israel responds by obediently following His commands, they experience shalom.

IMAGE-BEARER: MOSES

I review my notes out loud, not because I need them—the requirements are engraved on my mind like the tribes' names on Aaron's breastplate, which is waiting for my inspection among the mass of items—but because I want Bezalel, Ohliab, and every other craftsman here to take these instructions seriously.

Not seriously.

Solemnly.

Israel has been delivered from the clutches of Egypt and redeemed for this singular purpose: to be His people, His first-born among the nations, His chosen ones. Though, with the way they acted when we first fled Egypt, you wouldn't have thought so. Not only did they refuse Yahweh's invitation to come into His presence and instead sent me up alone, while I was receiving Yahweh's terms for the covenant and the instructions for this tabernacle (His solution, might I add, to dwelling with a people that feared Him), they gave into the lies of their fear and broke the first two terms of the covenant: worship only Yahweh and make no idols.

Yahweh had every right to back out of His covenant. He called them a stiff-necked people, ready to be done with them, and rightly so! What good is an animal that refuses to yield to its yoke and do what it has been distinctly made to do?

But, He didn't back out.

He could have simply kept his covenant with our forefathers by sending us away from Him into the Promised Land without Him.

But, He didn't.

No, He was merciful and gracious, slow to anger, abounding in loyal-love and faithfulness. And, just as He forgave our forefathers for their various sins, He forgave our failure to meet His standard, our rebellion against His boundaries, and our perversion of our image-bearer identity.

And so, not because we are special in our own right, but because He is Yahweh, He has taken us as His inheritance. He will be our God and His presence will dwell among us.

A solemn event, indeed.

"We have met the specifications for the ark."

I look up from my notes and meet Bezalel's eyes at his announcement. "Even the positioning of the cherubim on the mercy seat?" I ask, glancing towards the ark.

"Yes. Their wings cover the seat and their faces are positioned towards the seat. Even though, if I can be frank, Moses—" his voice halts but his eyes (surrounded, I note, by deeper wrinkles than nine-months ago) move back and forth searching for permission to voice his concern.

"Speak." I lean on my staff for support. Bezalel is not the only one affected by hard labor these days.

His hand motions to the golden box before us. "I don't know exactly what they look like. I was not there, in the Garden when the exile took place, I mean…"

Chuckles at the absurdity of the thought erupt from the craftsmen around us. A smile tugs at the corners of my own lips and compassion springs to my heart. I needn't have worried; Bezalel is doing enough for the both of us. I raise a hand to quiet the men and address Bezalel. "What did Yahweh say when He chose you to lead the construction?"

Bezalel looks away from me to the pile of items awaiting inspection and confirmation. Ohliab fills in the answer for Bezalel: "He called us by name, appointed us, and filled us with the Spirit of God so we could make all that He commanded."

I nod. "Yes, exactly. Look up, Bezalel."

He obeys.

"What Yahweh did not specify in His command, He empowered by His spirit the knowledge and intelligence to devise. Do not doubt. Do not fear."

Bezalel pulls his shoulders back. "Yes, Moses. And yes, they are positioned correctly."

We resume our diligent review of each commissioned item and its unique and detailed specifications, a reminder that Yahweh is holy, His dwelling place will be holy, and His people will be holy.

***

"It is all ready. They have completed all the work you commanded."

I sit before Yahweh in the Tent of Meeting, pride radiating through every nerve, muscle, and fiber of my being. These stiff-necked people have been obedient to their master's guidance, to the yoke placed on them. They have worked according to their purposed design, creating with and for Yahweh, bringing order to the chaos and beauty into design. In the faithful execution of His commands, they have rejected pharaoh's claim over their lives and fully embraced their identity as the people through which Yahweh will bless the nations.

I feel like a giddy little boy, overcome with excitement and anticipation.

Yahweh's pleasure punctuates His words as He instructs me to erect the Tabernacle on the first day of the first month of the second year.

I grin at the significance: A new beginning for Yahweh to do a new thing.

***

As I enter the courtyard with the entire congregation of Israel to meet Aaron and his sons, a flicker of concern passes across his face. It is so quick that I wonder if I had truly seen it.

When Yahweh first explained that Aaron and his sons would serve as His tabernacle priests, Aaron as the high priest, I wondered about the choice of man. I love my brother, but it was under his hand that the golden calf was crafted as a god at the request of the people.

I will forgive iniquities, Yahweh had reminded me and I never questioned His selection again.

But I wonder if Aaron questions it? It is hard to stand this close to Yahweh's presence and not be aware of all you lack.

This morning marks the eighth day since Yahweh's presence took up residence within the tabernacle, and yet, the sight of it is no less awe-provoking.

The first day of the first month of the second year, just as Yahweh commanded, the people gathered to help me raise the frame of the tent (making certain the entrance faced east), placed the testimony tablets inside the ark, set the mercy seat above the ark, screened the ark with a veil, and placed the furniture in their ordered places. We arranged the 12 loaves of the bread of presence into two stacks of six on the table, and filled each of the seven branches of the lamp with oil, burnt fragrance on the golden altar situated in front of the veil, and hung the curtain door to the tabernacle. We then set up the altar for burnt offerings and positioned the basin between the tent and the altar and filled it with water. I instructed Aaron and his sons to join me in washing our hands and feet. I offered the burnt offering and the grain offering before instructing the people in raising the courtyard wall around the tabernacle and altar. We hung the curtain gate at the entrance to the courtyard.

Every last detail was addressed and the work finished.

We waited, every man, woman, and child frozen in place—a mix of anticipation and fear holding us there.

Just when we were tempted to wonder if something was wrong, a cloud covered the tent and the glory of Yahweh filled every corner of it.

Excitement pulsated throughout my body. Finally, these people would experience Yahweh the way I did. His presence would dwell here with us. He had lovingly and graciously come down to His people when they were afraid to go up to Him.

I pulled the curtain gate aside and rushed forward past the altar and basin, desiring to sit face to face with Yahweh in this new dwelling.

But, at the entrance, I stopped abruptly.

I could feel it in my body—deep within my bones and the blood pulsing through my veins—the warning to come no nearer.

This sacred ground was not built for me to meet with Yahweh but for Yahweh to dwell with Israel. And the relationship between Yahweh and His people was not right.

Anoint, consecrate, and dedicate came the command.

With Israel assembled at the entrance of the tabernacle to watch, I anointed it and all within it. I sprinkled the anointing oil on the altar seven times. I dressed Aaron and his sons in the priestly garments.

Aaron and his sons placed their hands on the bull for a sin offering. The bull's life blood was spilled out for them. We repeated this laying on of hands with a ram for the burnt offering. We repeated it again with another ram, but this time for the purposes of ordination. I took the blood of the ram and put it on the lobe of Aaron's right ear, the thumb of his right hand, and the big toe of his right foot. I did the same for his sons.

A wave offering was completed next by placing pieces of the ram on the thick and thin loafs of bread. Aaron and his sons waved them as a wave offering. I took the breast of the ram, my portion of the ordination ram, and waved it for a wave offering.

Lastly, I took some of the anointing oil and the blood on the altar and sprinkled it on Aaron, his sons, and their priestly garments.

"Now," I addressed them, "you will stay here in this tent of meeting for seven days, doing all the Lord has charged so you do not die, until your ordination is complete.

They did all the things that the Lord had commanded.

Which is why Israel stands before them on this, the eighth day, ready with their offerings. The pivotal time has come. The sanctuary has been created and consecrated. Those who are to tend to it have been ordained. It is no longer about preparation. It is about action.

Atonement.

I turn in a circle slowly, taking in the people gathered around me. "This ceremony," I explain, "is a command from Yahweh so that you can see His presence dwelling with us."

I face Aaron once more. He nods to me, a signal he is ready to perform his duty as high priest.

"Draw near and make atonement for yourself and for the people." I motion towards the altar.

His movements are assured and precise as he sacrifices first the bull for the sin offering and then the ram for the burnt offering. He does it exactly as Yahweh instructed me and I instructed him. A little tinge of brotherly pride forms in my heart.

Next, Aaron offers the male goat for a sin offering on behalf of the people. Then their burnt offerings of a calf and lamb. The grain offering was burned as well.

So far, so good. The last thing for Aaron to perform is the peace offering. I notice my chest rising and falling quickly with short breaths as the anticipation grows within me.

Aaron kills the ox and the ram brought by the people to the tabernacle exactly as he should. His sons hand him the blood and he throws it against the sides of the altar. He lays the fat pieces from the ox and the ram and burns these rich pieces of the animals for Yahweh as is His due. The breast and right thighs, he waves as a wave offering.

Exactly as commanded.

Aaron puts the breast and the leg down and pauses with awe, and perhaps with a little relief that all has been done as it should. He raises his hands out over the people and blesses them.

He steps down from the altar and joins me. "Ready?" he asks.

"Yes." I answer with a huge smile.

Together we enter the tent of meeting and into Yahweh's presence.

Overwhelming and comforting. Convicting and forgiving. Freeing and calling.

Holy. Holy. Holy.

After what feels like seconds but is much longer than that, we rejoin Israel out in the courtyard with words to bless them.

We stand in the middle of the congregation, Aaron and I, and he raises his hands once more and utters the blessing Yahweh has given him to speak over the people:

"The Lord bless you and keep you; The Lord make His face shine upon you, and be gracious to you; The Lord lift up His countenance upon you, and give you peace."

With the final word, *shalom*, rolling off Aaron's lips, the glory of Yahweh fills the place where His people stand and a divine fire consumes the burnt offering and the pieces of fat on the altar.

Screams fill my ears and the sight of the people dropping to the ground and covering their faces fill my eyes.

But, I do not scream. I do not drop. I do not worry. Because He is near. Atonement has been made. The covenant upheld. We are His people.

Yahweh dwells with us once more.

Shalom has been restored.

And through us, all nations will have peace.

Day Four | Dwell on these Scriptures

READ EXODUS 34:1-10; EXODUS 20:8-11; DEUTERONOMY 5:12-15; EXODUS 25:1-9 through one time.

Reread these passages with the following in mind:

As you read, consider how, regardless of the Israelite's actions, God faithfully keeps His covenant (His promise) with humanity. He mercifully and graciously forgives Israel's forefathers, their generation, and the generations that would follow them. God's forgiveness does not depend on their obedience to the Ten Commandments or even the sacrifices offered later on. However, experiencing the wholeness God has for them (and for us) does require obedience to His commands.

Consider how this wholeness corresponds with 1) the presence of God and 2) the works He does with Israel and through them (Exodus 34:9-11).

As you read, consider how the Ten Commandments sum up these two concepts. The first three commands correspond to our relationship with God, to regard God as holy and deserving of all honor.

Consider how commands five through ten address the way we relate to the world around us. They command Israel to be the image-bearers they were made to be.

As you read, consider how the fourth is the only command given in a positive tone, urging action rather than restraint. It is also the only command that includes both honoring God and reflecting Him as His image-bearer.

Consider how the rationale for the command varies between Exodus, which highlights the creation narrative, and Deuteronomy which focuses on Israel's redemption from Egypt. These two are tied to one another. Through their deliverance, God removed their slave identity and reinstated their identity as His representatives on earth.

As you read, consider that Exodus prompts Israel to "remember" (*zakor*, to recall) their image-bearer identity, while in Deuteronomy, the new generation is instructed to "observe" (*samor*, meaning to guard or pay attention to), echoing the duty bestowed upon Adam in the garden. In fact, the creation narrative was vastly represented in the tabernacle design.

Consider how, traditionally, Jews wish each other *Shabbat shalom* each Sabbath. When we embody the posture of Sabbath—that is, worshiping God and reflecting Him, fully depending on His faithful provision as we do—we experience *shalom*.

Day Five | Dwell on this Theme

Redeemed Peace
God's redemptive plan prioritizes our complete well-being, our peace.

> If you walk in My statutes and keep My commandments so as to carry them out... I shall also grant peace in the land... Moreover, I will make My dwelling among you, and My soul will not reject you. I will also walk among you and be your God, and you shall be My people. I am the Lord your God, who brought you out of the land of Egypt so that you would not be their slaves, and I broke your yoke and made you walk erect. Leviticus 26:3-13 (NASB)

Redemption. Deliverance. Salvation. We often use these words interchangeably when referring to the exodus story, but they actually refer to three different ideas. Let's break it down:

Imagine you are walking along a river and the bank gives out, propelling you down and into the waters that are moving by at a crazy speed. Someone suddenly yanks you out! That awesome moment of rescue? That's "deliverance". Now, let's say the person who saved you had to give up their super rare limited-edition sneakers to do so. That sacrifice they made is the "redemption" part. And "salvation"? Well, it's the whole story from start to finish — one minute you're being carried by the current, then thanks to someone's brave act and their sacrificed sneakers, you're now chilling safely on the riverbank.

Within the Christian community, we often talk of Christ's redemptive work of the cross similar to the river example I just gave. His death involved an immense amount of suffering and pain, a sacrifice in every way. It had, however, another layer to it, one that we see much more clearly in the exodus story. Because, if you think about it, God's redemption of Israel didn't require sacrifice, but He still is their redeemer:

> Say therefore to the people of Israel, 'I am the Lord, and I will bring you out from under the burdens of the Egyptians, and I will deliver you from slavery to them, and I will redeem you with an outstretched arm and with great acts of judgment.'
> Exodus 6:6 (ESV)

Why not just deliver? Why redeem? The answer is found in the next verses:

> 'I will take you to be my people, and I will be your God, and you shall know that I am the Lord your God, who has brought you out from under the burdens of the Egyptians. I will bring you into the land that I swore to give to Abraham, to Isaac, and to Jacob. I will give it to you for a possession. I am the Lord.' Exodus 6:7-8 (ESV)

The definition of *redeem* is to buy back, repurchase, to get or win back.[7] Looking up the Hebrew word for *redeem* used in verse 6, we find the word *ga'al*[8], which means (you guessed it) to buy back. It also means to act as a kinsman-redeemer.

Now, if you have been a Christian for a little bit of time, you probably have been introduced to the story of Ruth and Boaz.

In ancient Israel, the concept of redemption related to the practice of buying back land or persons (like in the case of slavery). If someone sold themselves into slavery due to debt, a kinsman could "redeem" or buy back that relative from slavery. Similarly, if family land was sold, a kinsman had the right to buy it back to keep it within the family.[9] In other words, a kinsman-redeemer acted on behalf of a relative who was in trouble, danger, or need.

Ruth was in need; she was a foreigner whose husband and son had died, leaving her poor and with no ability to claim their family's land. Boaz was a relative who could provide, protect, ensure her place among God's people, and claim back her land by acting as her kinsman-redeemer.

Boaz had the ability to redeem Ruth's life back into *shalom*, a state of well-being, a state of safety and wholeness, by marrying her. Naomi, Ruth's mother-in-law, understood this. In Ruth 3:1, she says to Ruth, "My daughter, should I not seek rest for you, that it may be well with you?" The word *rest* here is the word *shalom*.

In Ruth and Boaz's story, we see echoes of the exodus story in which God is a relative of Israel (their creator/father) who can both prove His rightful claim and buy them back from Pharaoh (via the ten plagues and red sea) in their time of need (slavery, destitution) so that they can reclaim their inheritance (the Promised Land) and have *shalom*.

And in the story of Jesus we see echoes of Ruth and Boaz's story—quite literally as they are direct ancestors of His. Jesus is our relative (God's son) and in our time of need (slavery to sin) proves His rightful claim and buys us back from sin (via His death and resurrection) so that we can reclaim our inheritance (dwelling and co-ruling with God) and have *shalom*.

> Boaz had the ability to redeem Ruth's life back into shalom, a state of well-being, a state of safety and wholeness, by marrying her. Naomi, Ruth's mother-in-law, understood this. In Ruth 3:1, she says to Ruth, "My daughter, should I not seek rest [shalom] for you, that it may be well with you?"

Not only does Micah prophecy that Jesus would be from the line of David (who was Boaz's great-great-grandson) and that He would be born in Bethlehem (where Boaz redeems lands for Ruth). But, even more beautiful is the second part of this prophecy where Micah describes Jesus as a strong protector of his people, giving them a safe and secure dwelling place with Him.

"And he shall be their peace..." Micah 5:5a.

We can live with this assurance: God's redemptive plan prioritizes our complete and whole well-being, our peace.

Day Six | Dwell on this Question

Do I truly believe that the redemptive work of Jesus' death and resurrection has brought shalom to my relationship with Him and to my life?

JOURNAL YOUR RESPONSES to the questions below:

In the past, how have I defined peace?

When did I feel peace in my life? When did I experience *shalom*?

Do I truly believe that the redemptive work of Jesus' death and resurrection has brought *shalom* to my relationship with Him and to my life?

What part of this concept of *shalom* do I struggle with the most?

Take a moment to write out your personal confession of peace.

WEEK FOUR
GOD DWELLS WITH US
IN THE MESSIAH

WEEK THREE | OVERVIEW

ADVENT SUNDAY/SABBATH

Dwell with God: In Joy

DAY ONE

Dwell on these Scriptures: Psalms 105

DAY TWO

Dwell on these Scriptures: Psalms 106

DAY THREE

Dwell on this Truth: When we give God His proper role in our lives as the Creator God, and we embrace our proper role as His image-bearers, *shalom* is restored and joy is our response.

DAY FOUR

Dwell on these Scriptures: Psalms 84

DAY FIVE

Dwell on this Theme: Deeply-rooted Joy—When we dwell with God and follow His commands, we discover a deep joy anchored in His *shalom*, unshaken by life's challenges. (Psalms 16:11)

DAY SIX

Dwell on this Question: Do I allow this deeply-rooted joy to infiltrate my life?

Advent Sunday I Dwell with God in Joy

PREPARE

Candle Set & Lighter
JOY Ornament or Candle Label (if using)
Bible

Set aside distractions during this time of worship, reflection, and remembrance. Focus your thoughts on the joy that is anchored in the *shalom* we experience within God's presence.

As you light the CHRIST CANDLE, read John 1:1-3 out loud:

> In the beginning was the Word, and the Word was with God, and the Word was God. He was in the beginning with God. All things were made through him, and without Him was not anything made that was made.

REFLECT

Light the HOPE and PEACE CANDLES to remind you of the complete peace that comes from following your faithful God. You will light the JOY CANDLE today (also sometimes called the Shepherd Candle). As you do, reflect on the following:

Eventually, God brought Israel out of the desert into the promised land. Humans were designed to be co-rulers, but Israel begged God for a king like other nations, and He responded to their request. Some kings would do well in leading the nation towards God, like David who brought the tabernacle to Jerusalem and Solomon who built the temple as a reminder of God's presence with Israel. But, others would pull Israel away from Him, leading to their exile from Jerusalem.

From the examples of those who lived before us, we learn that to dwell in God's presence and to follow His commands, brings not only the *shalom* we talked about before, but also a deep joy. King David often wrote of the joy that comes from dwelling with God in his poetry and songs. Probably, one of the most famous of these is Psalm 23 in which He describes God as a shepherd who delivers in times of trouble, provides for our needs in abundance, and gives a dwelling place with Him for eternity. Later, Jesus would echo Psalms 23 as He called Himself the Good Shepherd who delivers, provides abundant life, and gives an eternal dwelling place with Him.

We light the JOY CANDLE to remember that joy is more than just a feeling of happiness that can come and go. It is resolute and lasting because it flows out of the *shalom* we have as we dwell with God and follow His commands.

Please light the JOY CANDLE at this time.

We read scripture to be reminded of God's truth. In Psalms 16 (whose author was also King David), we read about the joy that we have from dwelling with God. Read this portion of Psalms 16 (VOICE):

> Protect me, God, for the only safety I know is found in the moments I seek You. I told You, Eternal One, "You are my Lord, for the only good I know in this world is found in You alone."... I will bless the Eternal, whose wise teaching orches-

trates my days and centers my mind at night. He is ever present with me; at all times He goes before me. I will not live in fear or abandon my calling because He stands at my right hand. This is a good life—my heart is glad, my soul is full of joy, and my body is at rest. Who could want for more? You will not abandon me to experience death and the grave or leave me to rot alone. Instead, You direct me on the path that leads to a beautiful life. As I walk with You, the pleasures are never-ending, and I know true joy and contentment.

REJOICE

If you have a JOY ornament or a candle label, you may add it to your tree or candle at this time. When you see it there, may it remind you of the JOY that flows out of the peace we experience when we dwell with God.

Take a moment to give thanks:

> Father God, thank You for Your desire to dwell with us. Thank You for the JOY we experience in our lives as we dwell with You. As this week unfolds, may I remember that joy is not an emotion that comes and goes when we are happy, but is lasting because Your presence brings shalom peace. Amen.

Throughout this Advent season, we will be introduced to generations who cried out "Come, our Lord, come!" while waiting for the Messiah. Today, we remember that Jesus is that Messiah and that He will one day return to redeem and make right the world. As you close this time of reflection and rejoicing, add your voice with those generations before and pray:

Come, Lord Jesus, come.

Day One | Dwell on these Scriptures

READ PSALM 103 through one time.

Reread the passage again with the following in mind:

Many of the poems within the book of The Psalms (including this one) were written by David whose life was often fraught with challenges and strife. Additionally, many of these poems were used by the Temple's choir as part of their worship.

As you read, consider how it portrays joy as an attitude of praise anchored in the *shalom* of God, rather than a feeling that can come and go.

As you read, consider the poetic nature of this passage of scripture. If you are able, read it out loud, paying attention to the punctuation and line breaks.

Consider how the opening lines instruct David's whole being to bless God. Looking at the end of the poem, notice how all of creation (both heavenly and earthly) is instructed to bless the Lord, including David's soul.

As you read, note the attributes of God that are listed.

As you read, note the wondrous works of God that He has completed.

As you read, note the mentioned promises concerning how God will deal with His people.

Consider the implications of verses 10-12 for humanity as a whole and for you personally.

As you read, consider what this poem reveals about God's character and how that ties to the command to all of creation to praise Him.

Day Two | Dwell on these Scriptures

READ PSALM 105 through one time.

Reread the passage with the following in mind:

Note: While the psalm itself does not specify an author, it begins similarly to 1 Chronicles 16:8-22, which is part of a psalm David delivered when the Ark of the Covenant arrived in Jerusalem. Given this connection, some scholars believe David could be the author of at least part of this psalm or that the psalm was influenced by David's song.

As you read, consider the poetic nature of this passage of scripture. If you are able, read it out loud, paying attention to the punctuation and line breaks.

Consider how the first and last stanza bookend the middle section of the poem with a command to sing praises to Him and to tell of His wondrous works.

Consider how the first and last stanza mirror each other.

As you read, pay attention to the retelling of Israel's history. What do you notice?

Consider the cyclical nature within the retelling: first there is difficulty, then God delivers the Israelites from that difficulty.

Consider how the middle section serves as the rationale for the command to praise. What is the argument for praise being made here?

As you read the poem, make a note of all the attributes of God mentioned.

As you read the poem, make a note of all the ways in which God provided for Israel.

Day Three | Dwell on this Truth

When we give God His proper role in our lives as the Creator God, and we embrace our proper role as His image-bearers, shalom is restored and joy is our response.

IMAGE-BEARER: THE SERVANT GIRL

It was the sight of Michal that brought a smile to David's lips.

The insinuation behind her question "Are you proud of yourself?" stole it away just as quick.

She met our large group of revelers in the courtyard entrance, her own group of servants trailing behind her like a long robe trying to keep up with her quick pace. I think David's own excitement upon seeing her had led him to believe that her haste was from a similar excitement of her own.

I understand why he thought that; since the day Michal rejoined David as his wife, they have spent hours together, making up for the time taken from them by the cruelty of Saul. David has many wives and concubines, but Michal is the wife of his youth and holds a special place in his heart. Perhaps that is why she felt she could accost him in the courtyard with the intensity of a prophet. She didn't even bother to bow when she approached.

Standing tall before David with regalness, Michal reminds all present that she is both the daughter of a king and the wife of one.

David surveys the stance of his wife before taking a step towards her, his arms open in welcome towards her. "We missed you at the dedication."

She takes a step back from him to dodge his embrace. "Oh, did you? How could you have found the time to miss me?" She crosses her arms. "You were so busy *dancing*." Sarcasm drips from each word and a flourish of her hand underscores the last one.

David's outstretched hands drop to his sides and ball into fists. He doesn't break his gaze with Michal as he addresses the closest guard. "Ishmaiah, will you please lead our party to the hall for our feast? I need to speak with my wife for a moment." He relaxes his clenched fists.

"Yes, my king." Ishmaiah responds before taking the group's lead. His job, however, is an easy one; the group, unified in their desire to escape the building tension, part like a sea and weave their way around the pair. Sensing the hesitation of her servants behind her, Michal releases them with a nod.

I obediently follow the crowd forward. My place at the back means I will be one of the last to pass this scene of tension. Surely, they will wait to have this "conversation" until we have all taken our leave, won't they?

I discover the answer soon enough, as David only waits for his guards, wives, concubines, and children to file past him before launching into the conflict. In full sight of the servants, David commands Michal, "Say what you came here to say."

Without missing a beat, she responds, "You, o' king of Israel, have honored yourself today."

I know I should keep my eyes in front of me, but something compels me to look at Michal as she speaks. She notices my attention on her and, breaking her regal stance, rushes forward with purpose and grabs my arm. The servants next to me pause in surprise but quickly regain their composure and shuffle away—leaving me in the middle of the conflict. They know their place and it is not here.

Michal's nails dig into my skin as she drags me over to David. I immediately drop my head in a bow. "Straighten up, girl." Michal orders.

I hesitate. I know that as a servant I have no place ignoring Michal's command, but David is my king; it is out of respect for him that I disobey her.

Michal repeats the order.

"Do as she requests." The King says gently.

Michal jerks my arm before releasing it. I resist the urge to rub the skin irritated by her tight grip.

She takes a step away from me and motions towards her husband with a sweep of her hand. "Behold, mighty King David," she turns to me with a sneer, "forgetting his place among his people."

It is David's turn to cross his arms. The motion draws Michal's attention to the linen ephod he wears. Slowly, she approaches him, as if the garment has cast a trance over her. She reaches out and strokes the brightly woven threads. Her words are quiet but sharp: "Mighty King David, lowering himself to that of a common priest before his people."

He grabs her wrist. "Before God," he corrects, removing her hand from his chest and placing it on her own, directly over her heart. "Have you forgotten Him, our Savior, who did mighty things in Egypt?"

I sneak a glance behind me. Besides the three of us, the courtyard is completely empty. The entrance to the hall is not that far away. A quick pace would remove me from this awkward situation within moments.

As if reading my thoughts, Michal reaches out and places a hand on my shoulder to stop my exit while keeping David's gaze with her own.

"Tell us," Michal's hand drops from my shoulder to my back, "what did you think of your king's actions today? Did they make you proud? Or perhaps," she puts her lips near my ear and whispers teasingly, "did they make you blush with desire?"

I am not prepared for her words. Nor am I for the push she gives me and so, while it is not a strong one, it propels me towards the king. He catches me before I crash into him.

While the shock of Michal's words did not bring the heat to my face, the shock of the king's arms did the trick. I drop my face to hide the pink that I am certain colors my cheeks.

Once he is certain that I have regained my balance, David whips around to Michal and quickly closes the distance between them. "Have you forgotten yourself?"

Michal does not shrink back from his towering presence and even dares to poke a finger sharply into his chest. "No, you have!" Disgust wraps around each cold word like a coat. "You are the king! You have conquered the lands, united the tribes, and built this city. You are no longer that shepherd boy that came to live in my father's palace. You are King David. And yet, you danced like you had no claim to any of it today! Like you were unworthy. My father—"

"Your father!"

Michal and I both visibly jump at David's exclamation.

"Your father!" He repeats before balling his hands into fists and resting them on top of his head. He leans his head back and a yell of frustration violently escapes his body as if it has been hiding there for a very long time.

His fists tap the top of his head as he surveys his wife's face, waiting to see if she will take it back.

But she doesn't.

I want to run—I don't belong here in this intimate moment of conflict between husband and wife, especially when it is the king—but my legs won't work.

David sighs. "Your father failed. God chose me to be king instead of your father. He gave me the care and rule of Israel. No man did that, God did. Without Him, I am nothing! He deserves all the honor and praise. That is why I needed to bring the Ark of the Covenant here into this city. You know what happened the first time we tried. We ignored the commands about moving the Ark and it cost Uzzah his life." He beat his chest. "That is on me. I should have known that the Holy God demands the vessel of His presence to be treated with reverence and obedience."

"Don't you think it was all a bit extreme?"

"Excuse me?"

"The sacrifices every seven steps, the singing, the trumpets, the horns, cymbals, harps, and lyres? And then giving away all that food to the people? And the dancing! David, you looked ridiculous!"

"You say I have made a fool of myself before the people," David motions towards me, "that even the servant girl is ashamed of her king? But, I am saying that I have not lowered myself enough before God! I will celebrate before Him even more than I have done so today because I am unworthy of His steadfast love and provision. Everything I have, this entire household, is because of His favor. Do you hear me, Michal? I am His servant. He is my God."

The color drains from Michal's face. "You are serious."

David nods. "Your father disobeyed and it cost him God's favor. But, I tell you this: I will live my life humbled low before God in worship. And one day, even the servant girls," he doesn't bother to look at me this time, "will honor me because of it."

After so many words, the silence that falls between the two of them is unnerving. But it does its job of filling the cracks created by revelation.

He loves and worships the Creator.
She loves and worships the image.

David holds out a hand to his wife. "Will you join us for the feast?"

Michal shakes her head.

He drops his hand and I see grief flicker so quickly across his face. "Come," he addresses me.

With a respectful distance between the two of us, I follow the king. The frustration falls away from his shoulders and a posture of celebration returns with each step towards the hall, his family, and his worship.

When I pass Michal, I see on her face the same grief I saw briefly on David's. But her grief is mixed with anger, bitterness, and contempt.

David and Michal may have a history, but they no longer have a future.

He has a joy that flows from peace. She does not. Because of that, they will forever be at odds with one another.

And me? I have a new respect for this man who rules over me and my people. This man who worships God with such passion.

And he's right; I will honor him for it.

Day Four | Dwell on these Scriptures

READ PSALM 84 through one time.

Reread this passage with the following in mind:

As you read this psalm, you may recognize some of the wording it uses. Be careful not to skim over these familiar lines and, instead, consider them within the context of God's desire to dwell with humanity and co-rule with His image-bearers.

Consider that this psalm is broken into three stanzas, each followed by the word "Selah." Though its precise meaning remains elusive, the general consensus is that "Selah" serves as a marker to draw attention to or give emphasis to the accompanying text, signaling the reader or hearer to pause and reflect on the words of the psalm.

Consider the imagery presented throughout the psalm. What do you notice?

Consider how the sparrow is often used in scripture to illustrate the care and concern of God for even the smallest and most insignificant of creatures. How does that play a role in this psalm?

Consider how scripture often uses the swallow to symbolize restlessness or a longing for home. Notice how the line includes both the swallow and her young. How does this add a layer to the psalm?

As you read, consider how the Valley of Baca (it is uncertain if this is referencing a literal place or is being used metaphorically) is used to highlight provision God gives in the midst of challenges and the continued use of the phrase "blessed."

Consider how the doorkeeper's role had lowly status. Also, how the imagery of a court has a more permanent connotation than that of a tent. How does that underscore the psalmist's claim that dwelling in God's presence is precious?

Day Five | Dwell on this Theme

Deeply-rooted Joy
When we dwell with God and follow His commands, we discover a deep joy anchored in His shalom shalom, unshaken by life's challenges.

He is ever present with me; *at all times He goes before me.* I will not live in fear *or abandon my calling* because He stands at my right hand. *This is a good life*—my heart is glad, my soul is full of joy, and my body is at rest. *Who could want for more?* You will not abandon me to experience death and the grave or leave me to rot alone. *Instead,* You direct me on the path that leads to *a beautiful life.* As I walk with You, the pleasures are never-ending, and I know true joy and *contentment.* Psalm 16:8-11 (VOICE)

When Israel was too afraid to take God up on His invitation to ascend Mt. Sinai into His presence, God was gracious enough to come down from His exalted place to their lowly one and dwell among them. This is significant to our understanding of the loving and gracious character of God and His desire to dwell with His people.

Now, remember, God didn't just create the world for people to enjoy but for His image-bearers to partner with Him in tending to it and stewarding it. In other words, co-ruling with God. It is this dwelling-with partnership that God wants to redeem for humanity.

Throughout scripture, we get glimpses of the partnerships God makes with individual image-bearers to bring about His redemptive plan of blessing all the nations through Israel. David is one of those partners. God anoints David as a co-ruler of His people and appoints him to tend to them, as a shepherd does for a flock. One of his earliest acts as king is to bring the tabernacle into the city of Jerusalem and set it up on the highest elevated spot in the city so that the people can worship Yahweh there. Eventually, David desires to build a permanent house for God (a temple) but God gives that privilege to David's son Solomon once conflict with their neighboring nations has ceased.

And while God considered David "a man after my own heart" (1 Samuel 13:14), and he does a pretty good job of partnering with God in the tending of the nation of Israel as their shepherd-king, even David falls prey to the temptation of sin. But, he doesn't stay there. David's genuine sorrow for his sin and his desire to be reconciled with God are evident throughout the psalm, along with his deep joy anchored in the *shalom* that results from reconciliation.

Just as his father David did, Solomon started out as a strong partner with God, co-ruling Israel with God's wisdom, but crumbled to his own selfish desires. This—and other such rejection of God's commands by subsequent kings and God's people as a whole—had devastating results for Israel, eventually leading to destruction and exile. But, even then, God offered hope, both in the promise to return Israel to their home and to raise up a messiah who would bring salvation and redemption.

In the midst of their exile, God instructed Israel through Jeremiah to build homes, plant gardens, marry and have children, and then marry off those children so they could have children. In other words: make it your home. This instruction to be "fruitful and multiply" is an enduring echo for humanity. Stewardship of God's creation is a main component of our purpose (the first and foremost is to dwell with God, worshiping and honoring Him).

> God's desire for His people to experience wholeness and joy is not tied to a physical location but to His enduring nature.

In Jeremiah 29:7, He tells Israel to seek the *shalom* of the city because the well-being of that city would affect the well-being of Israel living in it. Later on, He tells them that His plans are for their good, their *shalom*. God's desire for His people to experience wholeness and joy is not tied to a physical location but to His enduring nature.

Daniel, Shadrach, Meshach, and Abednego, took this directive to heart and, within the context of exile, earnestly sought to dwell in God's presence, followed His commands, and prayed for the well-being of the city. Their lives were full of this deeply-rooted joy even in the midst of intense trials and hardships. God used these image-bearers to reflect Himself to King Nebuchadnezzar, bringing the ruler to eventually "praise, extol, and honor the King of heaven." (Daniel 4:37).

When we dwell with Him and follow His commands, we better understand who God is (His faithfulness, love, mercy) and His desires for us. We can rejoice in our current situations knowing He works all things together for our good, our *shalom*. That kind of joy is a natural response to dwelling with God, even in the midst of hardship.

Day Six | Dwell with this Question

Do I allow this deeply-rooted joy to infiltrate my life?

JOURNAL YOUR RESPONSES to the questions below:

When was the last time I was overwhelmed with joy by God's presence?

Is there unconfessed sin in my life that I need to bring to God for the sake of reconciliation and restoration of *shalom* and joy in my life?

Do I allow this deeply-rooted joy to infiltrate my life? Or do I give into the roller coaster of life with fear?

Do I struggle with this definition of joy? Why or why not?

Take a moment to write out your personal confession of joy.

WEEK FOUR
GOD DWELLS WITH US
IN THE MESSIAH

Week Four | Overview

ADVENT SUNDAY/SABBATH

Dwell with God: In Love

DAY ONE

Dwell on these Scriptures: Ezekiel 34; John 10

DAY TWO

Dwell on these Scriptures: Isaiah 52; 53

DAY THREE

Dwell on this Truth: God continually makes a way for salvation for His people, culminating in the Messiah's arrival.

DAY FOUR

Dwell on these Scriptures: Isaiah 9:2-3,6-7; Luke 1:67-79; Luke 2:1-38

DAY FIVE

Dwell on this Theme: Sacrificial Love—God dwelled with humanity as a human to atoned for our sins with His blood. (Romans 5:8)

DAY SIX

Dwell on this Question: Do I believe that Jesus redeemed my life with the loss of His?

CHRISTMAS DAY

Dwell with God: in Remembrance of Immanuel

Advent Sunday I Dwell with God in Love

PREPARE

Candle Set & Lighter
LOVE Ornament or Candle Label (if using)
Bible

Set aside distractions during this time of worship, reflection, and remembrance. Focus your thoughts on God's deep love for His creation and the salvation He extends to each of us.

In the past couple of weeks, you have started this time by lighting the CHRIST CANDLE and reciting the words of the apostle John:

> In the beginning was the Word, and the Word was with God, and the Word was God. He was in the beginning with God. All things were made through him, and without Him was not anything made that was made. (John 1:1-3)

Today, as you remember God's love towards the world and the coming of the Messiah, add the next few verses of John's gospel:

> In him was life, and the life was the light of men. The light shines in the darkness, and the darkness has not overcome it. (John 1:4-5)

REFLECT

Light the HOPE, PEACE, and JOY candles and remember the joy that flows out of the *shalom* peace that comes from following our faithful God. In a moment, you will light the LOVE CANDLE (also called the Angel Candle). As you do, reflect on the following:

Throughout the generations, Israel had a hope for the messiah, a deliverer from King David's family, who would bring peace and justice for God's chosen people. They had many ideas for what this Messiah would look like and act like, including the idea of the Messiah being a king who would dismantle the Roman occupation.

But, much like how Adam and Eve thought fig leaves would be enough to cover the sign of their rebellion, and how Israel demanded a king, the Israelites didn't fully understand what type of redeemer was necessary to restore humanity's identity and purpose as co-rulers, co-stewards, and co-creators with God and each other.

Only God could be that type of messiah. Only God could provide the necessary salvation. When the angel instructed Joseph to give the name Jesus to the baby Mary carried, it was a reminder of this very important truth. *Yeshua* (Jesus) means "God saves."

We light the LOVE CANDLE to remember how God's restorative plan doesn't depend on our understanding of it. Instead, it is because of God's love that He chooses to dwell with us and delivers us through His compassion, mercy, and grace. God saves because God loves.

Please light the LOVE CANDLE at this time.

We read scripture to be reminded of God's truth. In Romans 5:1-11, we read of the sacrificial love God has for us:

Therefore, having been justified by faith, we have **peace** with God through our Lord Jesus Christ, through whom we also have obtained our introduction by faith into this grace in which we stand; and we **celebrate in hope** of the glory of God. And not only this, but we also **celebrate in our tribulations**, knowing that tribulation brings about perseverance; and perseverance, proven character; and proven character, hope; and **hope** does not disappoint, because the **love of God** has been poured out within our hearts through the Holy Spirit who was given to us.

For while we were still helpless, at the right time Christ died for the ungodly. For one will hardly die for a righteous person; though perhaps for the good person someone would even dare to die. **But God demonstrates His own love toward us, in that while we were still sinners, Christ died for us.** Much more then, having now been justified by His blood, we shall be saved from the wrath of God through Him. For if while we were enemies we were reconciled to God through the death of His Son, much more, having been reconciled, we shall be saved by

His life. And not only this, but we also celebrate in God through our Lord Jesus Christ, through whom **we have now received the reconciliation**. Romans 5:1-11 (emphasis added)

REJOICE

If you have a LOVE ornament or label for your candle, add it at this time. May it remind you when you see it of the LOVE that God has shown humanity since day one of creation—especially, when He died on our behalf as the Messiah.

Take a moment to give thanks:

> Father God, thank You for Your desire to dwell with us. Thank You for the loyal LOVE you have faithfully had for each generation, a love that led you to sacrifice your life for our redemption. This week, may I live fully trusting that love. Amen.

Throughout this Advent season, we have been introduced to generations who cried out "Come, our Lord, come!" while waiting for the Messiah. Today, we remember that Jesus is that Messiah and that He will one day return to redeem and make right the world. As you close this time of reflection and rejoicing, add your voice with those generations before and pray:

Come, Lord Jesus, come.

Day One | Dwell on these Scriptures

Read Ezekiel 34 and John 10 through one time.

Note: These are two lengthy passages, but there is so much richness contained within them, I felt it was important to read the entirety of each passage.

Reread these passages with the following in mind:

As you read, consider how Ezekiel was a priest and a prophet during the time of the Babylonian exile, and how that underscores the decline of Israel's shepherds (any type of leadership for Israel, including the kings and religious leaders). Consider how Jesus' thinly veiled accusations of thievery and robbery towards the Jewish leaders echo God's accusation in Ezekiel that Israel's shepherds were preying on the sheep.

Consider how this imagery of a shepherd tending to the flock carries echoes of the creation account and the role of humans in caring for God's creation. This is not the first, and not the last, account of where an image-bearer tasked with partnering with God in co-stewarding has failed. God declares that He will step in where humanity has failed and take on the role of shepherd.

Consider how both God (in Ezekiel) and Jesus (in John) promise to retrieve that which belongs to Him and heal the sheep's wounds and neglect. Redemption and restoration.

As you read, consider this prophecy concerning the Messiah, a descendant of David and a true partner with God in caring for His sheep.

Keep this concept of God serving both as *the shepherd* and the *servant shepherd* in mind as you jump over to John 10.

Consider how Jesus promises that the sheep will find pasture in Him, just as God does in Ezekiel. Note the use of the phrase "life abundant" and "eternal life" by Jesus and how it parallels God's promise in Ezekiel that His sheep will dwell in peace.

Consider how Jesus promises to both lay down and take up His life for His sheep, an authority He has from God, echoing the imagery of both *the shepherd* and the *servant shepherd* in Ezekiel.

As you read, consider how this exchange happened during the Feast of Dedication (Hanukkah) which honored the deliverance of Jerusalem from oppression and the dedication of the second temple. Jesus was located physically in this temple when the Jews gather around Him.

Consider the shocking statement Jesus makes in John 10:38 that the Father is "in me and I am in the Father." The Greek word used for "in" is *en*. This is a word used to indicate a fixed position in place, time, or state.[10] Jesus uses this phrase to signify a mutual indwelling between Himself and God the Father. Jesus stands in the temple, claiming *to be* the temple of God.

As you read, note how the Jewish leaders understood Jesus claimed to be both God and the Messiah in this shepherd imagery and indwelling claim. They wanted Him to say so "plainly" so they could kill him for it.

Day Two | Dwell on these Scriptures

READ ISAIAH 52 AND 53 through one time.

Reread the passage with the following in mind:

As you read, consider the included imagery of Jerusalem enslaved, dirty, and sorrowful, arising with strength, removing her bonds, and adorning herself with beautiful garments, fully redeemed. A cause for celebration and joy.

Consider the phrase "how beautiful on the mountain are the feet of those who bring good new." Isaiah is referencing the idea of a messenger bringing news of victory or a herald making a royal announcement. The Greek equivalent for "good news" is "gospel."[11]

Consider the statement "you were sold for nothing, and you shall be redeemed without money" (verse 3). This redemption will require a different type of currency for the buy-back purchase.

Note how verse 12 echoes the exodus story but includes a plot twist. Where the Jews were warned their deliverance would be hasty, this time around, it is not. This suggests a peace that comes from knowing what God has accomplished in the past, He can do again.

As you read the rest of Isaiah 52 and chapter 53, look at how the servant will be prosperous and influential while also being rejected and considered inconsequential. He will be a descendant of King David, but He will not be considered a king by those around Him.

Consider the imagery of Israel as sheep scattering towards their own desires and wisdom, even their shepherds (political and religious leaders).

As you read, consider how God's servant, the Messiah, is one of the sheep (a human descendant of David, verse 2 refers to "the root of Jesse" prophesied earlier in Isaiah), the priestly shepherd offering the sacrifice, and the blameless lamb used in the sacrifice.

Day Three | Dwell on this Truth

Throughout the generations, God invited His people to dwell with Him as partners. Time after time, humanity rejected the invitation leading to their exile from the blessing of God's presence. But, God continually made a way for salvation, culminating in the Messiah's arrival.

IMAGE-BEARER: JOSEPH

Well, this is upsetting.

My father stands before me, expectantly. The answer seems simple enough to him; I should divorce Mary immediately.

But, not everything in Nazareth is simple. In fact, nothing in Nazareth is simple. We're a small town who keep to ourselves. Ourselves. And that's the problem. We don't worry about those outside our town, which gives us plenty of time to worry about those within it.

Too much time.

Three months in Mary's case. She has been gone for three months visiting her cousin, Elizabeth, in another town. Three months is a long time to speculate.

"Joseph?"

I raise my eyes from staring at my father's weathered sandals to his weathered face.

"She has broken the *ketubah*." My father reminds me.

I do not need to be reminded.

I also do not need to be reminded of Mary's beauty, both inside and out. Do not need to be reminded of Mary's deep brown eyes, eyes that give a glimpse into her soul—also beautiful. Nor do I need to be reminded of how Mary is desired by many.

Desired. Pursued. Sought after.

But, she was promised to me. A contact was drafted and signed. I presented her father with the *mohar*. Mary may be desired by many, but she is also bought with a price.

"I understand," I finally answer him. We stand in my home, the one I have crafted with pride for the last year since the *ketubah* was agreed upon. I finished this home just in time for the second part of our marriage, the wedding night, which is to take place next month.

"Then why do you hesitate? Let us go to the synagogue and present the bill of divorce."

"Father..."

"Will you let her disgrace you as she has disgraced herself? If you do not speak up now, all in Nazareth will think the child is yours. Your reputation will be ruined! Go now and put her to shame so that none is brought on your own head."

Upsetting isn't a strong enough word.

I *chose* Mary because of her beauty, her reputation, and her family.
I *love* Mary because of her strength, her laughter, and her intelligence.

Devastating is a much better word.

Love has blossomed in my heart. Scandal threatens to pick the flower and crush it underfoot.

Anger wells up inside me. "Do not command me as you would a child!"

My father's eyes widen at my outburst. He holds up a hand. "Do not speak with disrespect to me."

I try to calm my anger. "Forgive me, Father. But," I motion towards the neighboring houses, "how do you know that this news is not just a false rumor? One of the women may have started it. You know how malicious they can be." The words tumble out one on top of the other.

My father sighs. "Joseph, go to her yourself and see. And may your love not blind you to the truth."

With my father's words spurring me to action, I hastily exit my home, slowing only when I pass my neighbor. I force my steps into a normal gait, but it does nothing to keep the pitying glances at bay.

At the sound of my sandals on the rocks, Mary's mother looks up from where she is tending her garden. Realization first fills her face and then a hot shame replaces it as she pushes herself back on her heels and then stands from the ground to greet me.

"Joseph," she drops her eyes and bows her head, the pleading in her voice confirms my fears.

"Where is she, Sarah?" I ask, my stomach turning.

"She is inside. I will call for her if you insist, but…" she finally looks up at me and unexpectedly grabs my arms, "please, Joseph, be gracious to her. I understand should you choose to put her away, but," her voice becomes desperate and her grip tighter, "be merciful to her. Do not disgrace her anymore than she already has disgraced herself."

"Mother, do not plead for me."

Sarah drops her hands from my arms as we turn to the voice at the door of the house.

I first see Mary's beautiful brown eyes and then her form. She is obviously with child. I look back to her face and Mary's gaze holds mine.

"Mary –" I stop when my voice breaks.

"Joseph, it is not as it seems." She says calmly.

No, not just calmly. There is a hint of excitement in her words.

My skin prickles. Not as it seems? I want to vomit at the denial.

She takes a step forward, then remembering our situation, stops herself. She is a rule-follower. Mary knows the Torah as well as I do. We know the scriptures. We know the commands. She has always sought to follow the rules. I love her for it.

But it is hard to argue with a protruding stomach.

I open my mouth to speak, then close it. She moves a piece of hair back under her head covering. "What I say is true, please, I beg of you, let me explain."

I finally find my voice. "I need no explanation," I say, the sadness that tinges the edge of each word surprising me. "May God judge you appropriately. You have broken His command and you have broken our covenant. You answer to Him, as do I."

I break my gaze with Mary decidedly and turn to Sarah. "You can tell Nathan that I will not act as my due. I require only that he brings Mary to meet me at my home tomorrow evening so we may end our agreement quietly with witnesses. After that, I will be released from Mary and she will be free to do as she pleases."

Sarah nods her understanding, her gratitude clearly conveyed on her face.

"Joseph! Please, you do not understand. Please let me explain!" Mary tries to approach me, but Sarah steps to her side and leans close to her. "Do not speak, child," she instructs her in a quiet voice. "You have brought enough disgrace on yourself."

My retreat from their presence is as hasty as it was from my father's, only slowing when Mary's voice calls after me, her voice cracking as the bricks I work with do when they have been hit one too many times.

An intense desire to pull her into my arms and comfort her slams into my chest and threatens to steal the breath from my lungs. In an act of defiance, I inhale deeply and resume my quick pace.

Silence fills the space as I walk away from Mary and I am tempted to glance back to see if she is still there. But, I don't. I know she is. I know she stands there in her quiet strength, shoulders rolled back and head held high. I find myself almost wishing she would yell after me so I would have a reason to return to her.

So very upsetting.

***

"Joseph."

I flinch at the sound of my name.

"Joseph."

It is not familiar to me.

"Joseph."

The sternness of the tone strikes my confusion into clarity and I see him standing before me, an image of a man but not like any I have ever seen before. His form is fluid and made up of flashes of colored lights that swirl and twist and bounce within his being. There is a light that seems to come from deep within him, radiating out and yet reflecting from a source outside of him back in. As if the flame that burns within came from a fire elsewhere.

It confuses me and alarms me all at the same time and I drop to my knees and face.

"Joseph, son of David," comes the voice again, this time a little less stern and my fear abates enough for me to comprehend that I stand in the presence of one of Yahweh's messengers.

"Do not be afraid to take Mary as your wife. For the child within her was conceived by the Holy Spirit."

The Holy Spirit? My mind searches for something from earlier in the day. Something important. Suddenly it finds it: the excitement hidden behind Mary's restraint.

She knows.
She was trying to tell me.

"And she will have a son," the messenger continues.

A son! The baby inside her is a boy. It takes everything inside me to stay facedown out of respect when all I want to do is jump up and run to Mary's side.

The messenger is still speaking, so I will myself to focus on his words, not wanting to miss anything. A smile plays at the corners of his mouth as he instructs me, "And you are to name him Jesus, for he will save his people from their sins."

In a moment, both the messenger vanishes from my sight and my mind engages, waking me up from my dream state.

I sit up in my bed with a jerk.

Very upsetting, indeed... upsetting in the very best possible way.

Day Four | Dwell on these Scriptures

READ ISAIAH 9:1-7; LUKE 1:67-79, AND LUKE 2:1-38 through one time.

Note: Once again, there is quite a bit to read here, but there is so much to be gained from meditating on these scriptures!

Reread Isaiah 9:1-7 with the following in mind:

As you read verse 1, consider how this is a prophecy grounded in imagery of the exodus.

As you read verses 2-3, consider this imagery of a world covered in darkness, then a great light shines. Also, note the joy that follows God's favor in multiplying the nation and providing abundance. Both statements carry echoes of the creation story.

Consider, in verse 4-5, this reference back to the battle of Gideon (Judges 6-7) against the Midianites. Because of Israel's disobedience, God allowed the Midianites to ransack Israel's crops during harvest. Israel cries out to God. He raises up Gideon to destroy the altar of Baal (which means "master"), tear down the Asherahs (tree-like structures honoring the goddess of fertility), and defeat Midian in battle with only 300 men. This reference accomplishes two things: 1) calls to remembrance that God is the true Creator God who brings about abundant life, and 2) reminds Israel that they cannot break away from this oppressive master without God's divine and miraculous intervention.

As you read verse 6-7, be sure to slow down as you move through these very familiar verses. We often see these verses as describing the peace the Messiah will bring to a turbulent world. But, read this time with the references to creation, exodus, and the battle of Midian in mind. The messiah will *be God*, the eternal who was at the beginning of Creation. He has the both earthly right (a child born from King David's line) and divine right. He also has the ability to redeem His kingdom (His dwelling place with humanity) and restore *shalom*.

Reread Luke 1:67-79 with the following in mind:

As you read Zechariah's prophecy, consider how he echoes the prophecies of the psalms and prophets. Especially note the use of the phrases "horn of salvation", "servant David", and "give light to those who sit in darkness". Note the reference to the Abrahamic covenant and God's promise to bless the nations through Israel. Also, note the shepherd imagery of guidance to a place of *shalom*.

Reread Luke 2:1-38 with the following in mind:

Once again, you may be tempted to quickly read through the familiar account in Luke of Jesus' birth. As you read, bring all the themes and events we have been considering so far into the reading of this recorded account of the birth of Immanuel.

Consider how in the first few verses we get specific messianic imagery concerning Jesus.

1. He born in Bethlehem—a fulfillment of prophecy, and a reminder of the kinsman-redeemer

2. A descendant of David—an important requirement for the Messiah

3. A firstborn—firstborn humans and animals were dedicated to God's service (this point is repeated in verse 22)

4. He slept in the manger (a feeding place for animals)—God promised to feed His sheep in Ezekiel

Consider how the first to receive news of His birth are other shepherds and that the angels echo the words of Isaiah 9: a child, the suffering servant and prince of peace, has been born as a savior for us.

As you read, notice how it is on the eighth day, a day often associated with newness, or new creation, that the child is named Jesus, "God saves."

Consider the fact that Simeon (whose name means "God has heard"[12]) was waiting for the Messiah at the temple when Jesus was brought there to be consecrated to the Lord. He takes Jesus into his arms and also echoes Isaiah when he says, "my eyes have seen your salvation... a light to the Gentiles and for glory to your people Israel."

Consider how Anna, a prophetess, is also at the temple worshiping at the same time. When she sees Jesus, she breaks out in praise. She tells everyone who is waiting for the redemption of Jerusalem that Jesus is the Messiah. Her name means "grace or favor."[13] It is also a variation of the name Hannah, echoing the story of a woman who earnestly prayed for a child (Samuel) and fulfilled her promise to dedicate Him to the Lord's service.

Day Five | Dwell on this Theme

Sacrificial Love
When humanity chose to pursue their selfish desires instead of trusting their Creator, God sacrificially dwelled with humanity as the Messiah, atoning for our sins with His blood.

> When the time was right, the Anointed One died for all of us who were far from God, powerless, and weak." Romans 5:6 (VOICE)

It shouldn't have been necessary for God to take on the role of both Creator and image-bearer. His original design and desire was to share the joy of caring for His abundant provision. For this purpose, He created a cosmic tabernacle—a place where heaven and earth met in sacred harmony. He designed Adam and Eve to serve as His priestly representatives, ruling and stewarding alongside Him in the garden-kingdom.

Of course, Adam and Eve made a mess of things. But God, even when humanity rebelled against His commands and trusted their own wisdom, continued to make a way to dwell with His image-bearers. Again and again.

Dwelling with humanity as the Messiah was always the plan. It is tempting to read the narrative of the Bible as if God forgave sins one way (through sacrifices at the temple) and then a different way (through Jesus' death). But, I hope, as we have moved through these last few weeks, you have begun to see how God has always treated humanity's sinful disobedience the same way: with mercy, grace, compassion, forgiveness, and sacrifice.

I also hope you have begun to see that redemption is concerned with negating the claim of ownership by another (sin) and restoring identity (as an image-bearer of God), while reconciliation focuses on restoring purpose (dwelling with God as a co-ruler).

He did it for Adam and Eve in the garden. Even though they broke the terms of their covenant with God, He forgives them. He then provides for their needs physically (He clothes them) and spiritually (He shares His plan for redemption and sends them out of Eden), knowing that it will cost Him everything and them nothing.

He did it again for Abraham, Isaac, Jacob, and their descendants. He forgave their sins out of His loyal-love and merciful character. In the waiting for His redemptive plan, He made a way for reconciliation through trusting God's promises and obeying His commands, including animal sacrifices. Within that reconciliation, humanity, specifically Israel, was invited to dwell with God and co-steward with Him; Israel was invited to be His priestly representatives like Adam and Eve. Once again, it would cost God everything (His pending redemptive plan) and humanity nothing (the animal was sacrificed as a representation of God's ultimate sacrifice, not their sacrifice).

Humanity believed and trusted, but it cost them nothing holy and good to do so. True reconciliation requires sacrifice by the offender to make things right with the offended for what they lost *and* the assurance that the offense will not happen again.

> No matter how many times an individual, a priest, or a king offered a sacrifice on behalf of themselves and of the people to bring about reconciliation, it could not make a lasting impact because there was no accompanying assurance that the offense would never happen again.

The forgiveness of sins has always depended on the merciful and gracious character of God. The redemption of humanity has always depended on God's loyal-love of His creation. But true and lasting reconciliation required a sacrifice from the offender (humanity) that would right the wrong (sinful disobedience) committed against the offended (God) with an assurance the offense (sinful disobedience) would never happen again.

No matter how many times an individual, a priest, or a king offered a sacrifice on behalf of themselves and of the people to bring about reconciliation, it could not make a lasting impact because there was no accompanying assurance that the offense would never happen again.

On their own, the image-bearers could never offer that assurance because sin had corrupted their ability to faithfully obey the Creator. So, God became and accomplished that which we did not have and could not offer: the sacrifice of our sinless life.

He became both...

Creator and Created Image-bearer
The Offended and the Offender
Son of God and Son of Man

He also became...

The King and the Suffering Servant
The Redeemer and the Ransom
The Mediator and the Settlement Agreement
The High Priest and the Sacrifice
The Intercessor and the Restitution

We are God's people, the sheep of His pasture, and He loves us. He desires to be reunited with us. He took all these roles obediently to the cross and there exercised His kingly right to redeem His kingdom. But, in a plot-twist, He does so in order to share the rulership of His abundant provision with His image-bearers. Through the Messiah's loving sacrifice, humanity was redeemed and offered an everlasting reconciliation.

Day Six | Dwell on this Question

Do I believe that Jesus redeemed my life with the loss of His?

JOURNAL YOUR RESPONSES to the questions below:

When I think of the word "love" what first comes to mind?

When I think about God's love for me, what comes to mind?

Do I believe that Jesus is my redeemer who ransomed me from sin's claim with the costly price of His life?

What do I struggle to believe concerning Jesus' redemption and reconciliation of my life?

Take a moment to write out your personal confession of God's sacrificial love.

Christmas Day | Dwell with God in Remembrance of Immanuel

PREPARE

Candle Set & Lighter
NATIVITY Ornament or Candle Label (if using)
Bible

Set aside distractions during this time of worship, reflection, and remembrance. Focus your thoughts on Immanuel, God with Us.

REFLECT

Each week during this Advent season, we have started our time by lighting the CHRIST CANDLE while reciting the first three verses of the Gospel of John.

> In the beginning was the Word, and the Word was with God, and the Word was God. He was in the beginning with God. All things were made through him, and without Him was not anything made that was made. John 1:1-3

We purposely have done this because the story of Jesus didn't start in a little town in Bethlehem; it started back at Creation.

The same Creator who walked with Adam and Eve in the Garden, walked with John the disciple (and many others) in Israel. John describes it this way: "And the Word became flesh and dwelt among us, and we have seen his glory, glory as of the only Son from the Father, full of grace and truth." (John 1:14)

God first dwelled with His creation within creation, the cosmic tabernacle. Once that relationship was fractured and a redemptive plan was necessary, God dwelled with Israel in the desert, in the tabernacle built under the leadership of Moses, and in Jerusalem, in the temple built under the leadership of David and Solomon.

He used the people of Israel to point all nations to this very moment we celebrate today: the moment when He dwelled among humanity in a new temple built by God himself, the person of Jesus.

Jesus was both fully God and fully man, which means He was both God and the human image of God. He lived a life of humanity—experiencing temptation, suffering, and joy just as we do—but He did so without rebelling against God's commands, without sin. In Him, Heaven met Earth once again, a divine tabernacle within human form.

We light the CHRIST CANDLE today not just to remember the moment in time God became both fully God and fully man, but the astounding truth that He did so in order to fulfill the role of the Christ—the one anointed (chosen) to be our deliverer, our redeemer, and our kingly high-priest.

Please light the CHRIST CANDLE, HOPE CANDLE, PEACE CANDLE, JOY CANDLE, and LOVE CANDLE. As you light them, may these lights remind you of God's enduring desire to dwell with His people and His faithfulness to make a way for us to do so.

We read scripture to be reminded of God's truth. As you celebrate the birth of Christ today, read the rest of John's account:

In the beginning was the Word, and the Word was with God, and the Word was God. He was in the beginning with God. All things were made through him, and without him was not any thing made that was made. In him was life, and the life was the light of men. The light shines in the darkness, and the darkness has not overcome it.

There was a man sent from God, whose name was John. He came as a witness, to bear witness about the light, that all might believe through him. He was not the light, but came to bear witness about the light.

The true light, which gives light to everyone, was coming into the world. He was in the world, and the world was made through him, yet the world did not know him. He came to his own, and his own people did not receive him. But to all who did receive him, who believed in his name, he gave the right to become children of God, who were born, not of blood nor of the will of the flesh nor of the will of man, but of God.

And the Word became flesh and dwelt among us, and we have seen his glory, glory as of the only Son from the Father, full of grace and truth. John bore witness about him, and cried out, "This was he of whom I said, 'He who comes after me ranks before me, because he was before me.'" For from his fullness we have all received, grace upon grace... The next day, he [John] saw Jesus coming towards him, and said, "Behold, the Lamb of God, who takes away the sin of the world." (John 1:1-16,29)

REJOICE

If you have an ornament that portrays the nativity scene on it (or a candle label) you can add it to your tree at this time. May it remind you of the day that God was born as the Messiah in Bethlehem. *Immanuel.*

Take a moment to give thanks:

Father God, thank You for Your desire to dwell with us. Thank you for making a way for reconciliation through the Messiah's birth, life, death, and resurrection. Amen.

Throughout this Advent season, we have been introduced to generations who cried out "Come, our Lord, come!" while waiting for the Messiah. Today, you remember that Jesus is that Messiah. Today is a very *Merry Christmas* (a celebration of Christ's birth)!

Today you celebrate this first Advent of Christ remembering that He will one day return to redeem and make right the world. As you close this time of reflection and rejoicing, add your voice with those generations before and pray:

Come, Lord Jesus, come.

WEEK FIVE
GOD DWELLS WITH US
IN US

Week Five | Overview

ADVENT SUNDAY/SABBATH

Dwell with God: In Renewal

DAY ONE

Dwell on these Scriptures: Matthew 4:12-5:16; 1 Peter 2:9

DAY TWO

Dwell on these Scriptures: Isaiah 66:18-21; John 17:17-23; Eph. 2

DAY THREE

Dwell on this Truth: Through Jesus' redemptive work, a new creation tabernacle is built, the church of believers, in which the Spirit dwells.

DAY FOUR

Dwell on these Scriptures: Colossians 3:1-4:6; Ephesians 5:15-16

DAY FIVE

Dwell on this Theme: Ongoing Renewal. We are the Temple of the Holy Spirit. His presence does a work of renewal in and through our lives.

DAY SIX

Dwell on this Question: Do I live as if I believe I am a temple of God?

Advent Sunday I Dwell with God in Renewal

PREPARE

Candle Set & Lighter
CHURCH Ornament or Candle Label (if using)
Bible

Set aside distractions during this time of worship, reflection, and remembrance. Focus your thoughts on the renewing work the Spirit does on our lives as He dwells with us, empowering us to partner with God in renewing the world around us.

Begin by lighting the CHRIST CANDLE and reading John 1:1-5:

> In the beginning was the Word, and the Word was with God, and the Word was God. He was in the beginning with God. All things were made through him, and without Him was not anything made that was made. In him was life, and the life was the light of men. The light shines in the darkness, and the darkness has not overcome it.

REFLECT

Light the HOPE, PEACE, JOY, and LOVE CANDLES. Soon, you will light the RENEWAL CANDLE. As you do, reflect on the following:

Since the time of Adam's and Eve's rebellion, sacrifices had been made to temporarily reconcile Israel with God year after year. But, Jesus' death brought about a final atonement because he was all things necessary: the temple in which Heaven and Earth converged, the high priest representative for both God and man, the sacrifice from the offender to make the amends and assurance, the offended (God) judging the amends and assurance sufficient for the offense of creation's rebellion—past, present, and future.

We know His death is not where the story ended. Unlike Adam and Eve who were exiled from the garden and experienced death, Jesus rose from the dead three days later. He then appeared to his disciples and hundreds of others for 40 days before He ascended to Heaven with the promise He would one day return. Before He left, Jesus commanded His followers to represent Him to all nations, teaching them what it means to love Him and follow His commands. He also promised that while He would no longer dwell among them, the Spirit would.

Christ's resurrection signaled His power over death and His ability to renew the life of His followers for eternity, redeeming our purpose as God's image-bearers. The Apostles used phrases like "new creation" and "temple of the Holy Spirit" to describe believers, a place where Heaven meets Earth and God's Spirit dwells with humanity. The life of the believer becomes both the set-aside place for God to dwell and the thing to care for as co-stewards and co-rulers with God, becoming the very act of worship and sacrifice in the presence of God.

And the story continues. Our lives are being renewed through the presence of the Spirit more and more into the image of Christ while also being used to bring about the renewal of all of creation. Just as God gave the Israelites a way to dwell and work with Him while they waited in the wilderness to enter the Promised Land, God gives us a way to dwell with Him and work with Him while we wait for all of creation to be reconciled and renewed when Christ returns to dwell in this cosmic tabernacle with humanity once more.

Please light the RENEWAL CANDLE at this time.

We read scripture to be reminded of God's truth. In Titus 3:4-8, we read of the renewing work of the Spirit in our lives:

> But when the goodness and loving kindness of God our Savior appeared, he saved us, not because of works done by us in righteousness, but according to his own mercy, by the washing of regeneration and renewal of the Holy Spirit, whom he poured out on us richly through Jesus Christ our Savior, so that being justified by his grace we might become heirs according to the hope of eternal life. The saying is trustworthy, and I want you to insist on these things, so that those who have believed in God may be careful to devote themselves to good works. These things are excellent and profitable for people.

REJOICE

If you have a Renewal ornament or candle label, you can add it now. We know that the Church is not a building, but this symbol reminds us that God's Spirit dwells in believers and He is using us, all together, to bring others to Him.

Take a moment to give thanks:

> Father God, thank You for Your desire to dwell with us. Thank You for dwelling through Your Spirit in each of us as individuals and all together as the Church. Please continue to RENEW our lives, helping us to be more and more like Christ so that others can see our lives and believe in You. Amen.

Throughout this Advent season, we have been introduced to generations who cried out "Come, our Lord, come!" while waiting for the Messiah. Today, we remember that Jesus is that Messiah and that He will one day return to redeem and make right the world. As you close this time of reflection and rejoicing, add your voice with those generations before and pray:

Come, Lord Jesus, come.

Day One | Dwell on these Scriptures

READ MATTHEW 4:12-5:16 AND 1 PETER 2:4-5,9-10 through one time.

Reread Matthew 4:12-5:16 with the following in mind:

As you read, consider how Jesus' actions in this passage mirror Moses' story. He leaves the wilderness (there He was tempted by the devil and did not sin), establishes authority through signs and wonders, and leads a large group of people up a mountain to give them commands.

Consider how the series of "blessed are the" statements feel covenant-like. They speak of a blessing that flows out obediently aligning oneself with God's righteousness. It also hints at a "promised land" in phrases such as "kingdom of heaven", "inherit earth", and "reward in heaven."

Consider how Jesus references the prophets and how they were persecuted. The prophets were persecuted for living out their covenant relationship with God and reminding Israel to do the same.

Consider the prophecy from Isaiah quoted in this passage and how it refers to Jesus as the "light" that dawns on a people living in darkness. This imagery is repeated often by Jesus and the New Testament authors and echoes back to the creation story (darkness covered the face of the deep...and God said, "let there be light").

As you read, note the reference to "salt of the earth". Salt was used to preserve and keep in ancient times. It was used to make covenants between two parties and signified the intention for a long-lasting relationship. There are many layers to this statement, but for now, note the fact that salt was commanded to be included in grain offerings. Grain offerings were made with the finest elements and symbolized thanksgiving for God's provision and a dedication of a person's life and work to God.

As you read, consider the echoes in Jesus' statement regarding His followers: light of the world, a city on a hill, and a lamp. Throughout scripture, we read how when we follow The Light, we too become light to a dark world through the indwelling of the Holy Spirit (Eph 5:8). We are a tabernacle/temple that points the world to Jesus. As did the city of Jerusalem with the temple elevated in its center and the lampstand within the tabernacle casting light on the holy of holies.

Reread 1 Peter 2:4-5, 9-10 with the following in mind:

Consider this passage in relation to the passage in Matthew we just read. How does it parallel Jesus' sermon on the mount?

As you read, note the fact that Peter is talking to believing Jews who are dispersed throughout the Roman empire. He is reminding them of their history as Israelites while impressing on them their new identity and purpose as Christ followers.

Day Two | Dwell on these Scriptures

READ ISAIAH 66:18-21, JOHN 17:17-23, AND EPHESIANS 2 through one time.

Reread Isaiah 66:18-21 and John 17:17-23 with the following in mind:

Depending on what Christian tradition you have been part of, you may think that God's original choice was Israel but, when they continued to break their covenant with God, He decided to change His plan to include everyone. This is not Biblical.

As you read, consider how the prophets talked frequently about the day when every nation would worship God. They believed that in this moment, the covenant with Abraham would be fully fulfilled: to bless all the nations through Israel. When Jesus announces the start of His ministry, He reads from one such prophet: Isaiah.

As you read these verses in Isaiah, consider how there is both a gathering and a sending out of people on God's part. We see this in the life of Jesus as He calls people to follow Him and then sends them out as His witnesses (Matt 28:18-20).

Consider how Jesus' words in John are asking God to sanctify His followers. In some Bible translations it might be noted as *The High Priestly Prayer*. Here Jesus is consecrating Himself to the work of God, namely sacrificing His life. He also asks God to sanctify (set apart) believers for two reasons: 1) so that they can dwell intimately with God (temple) and 2) so that they could be image-bearers to the world so that they may believe in Jesus (priest).

Reread Ephesians 2 with the following in mind:

As you read, consider the imagery of a new creation presented. Believers are dead but are "raised up" with Jesus to new life.

In verse 10, the word translated as "workmanship" is the Greek word *poiema*.[14] It's the word from which we get the English word "poem."[15] It refers to something that has been made or crafted, essentially a "work of art" or "creation." Read this verse with this perspective: God is the poet writing poetry and our lives are the resulting poem.

Consider the insinuation that we are not just simply created, but created to co-rule. We are raised to a new life *and* seated with Jesus in the heavenly places. In ancient cultures, this idea of being seated was connected to royalty and authority.

Consider how verses 11-18 both echo Isaiah's prophecy and also emphasize this idea of a renewed humanity, no longer fractured but unified.

As you read, note how we are members of God's household, signifying that we dwell intimately with Him. This underscores other places in scripture (John 14 for example) where Jesus talks about God and Jesus making their home with those who love Him and keep His commandments (which echoes the Mosaic covenant).

Note how there is both an individual aspect of dwelling with God (members of His household) and a collective whole. While we are individual temples we are also part of a bigger temple being built together for God to dwell by the Spirit. In other places in scripture, it speaks to the ways the Spirit empowers each believing individual "priest" to care for the collective temple (the Church).

Day Three | Dwell on this Truth

Through Jesus' redemptive work, a new creation tabernacle is built, the church of believers, in which the Spirit dwells.

IMAGE-BEARER: SIMON PETER

Suddenly: the roar of a violent wind fills the house.
Next: a flame dividing and spreading to rest on each of us.
Then: the Spirit empowering.

"Follow me, Simon," He had said.
Fisherman, I was.
I will renew your work.
Fisher of men, I became.

"How do we hear our own native languages?" They ask.
"Aren't these Galileans?"

"Come out on the water," He had said.
Drowning, I was.

I will renew your faith.
Saved, I became.

        "What does this mean?" Some wonder.

"Who do you say I am?" He had asked.
Unsure, I was.
I will renew your perspective.
Certain, I became.

        "They are drunk." Some mock.

"Get behind me, Satan!" He had said.
Misdirected, I was.
I will renew your understanding.
Aligned, I became.

        "All who dwell in Jerusalem, give ear to my words,"
                I lift up my voice.

"Do you want to go away as well?" He had asked.
Lost, I was.
I will renew your belief.
Chosen, I became.

        "You crucified Jesus but God raised Him up," I say.

"Seven times seventy," He had answered.
Resentful, I was.
I will renew your heart.
Forgiving, I became.

        "Of this, we are witnesses," I say.

"Do you love me?" He had asked.
Fisher of men, I was.
I will renew your purpose.
A shepherd of the Church, I became.

        "What shall we do?" They ask.

"I will pour out my Spirit," He had said.
Denier, I was.
I will renew your words.
Proclaimer, I became.

        "Repent, be baptized in the name of Jesus Christ,
           and receive the gift of the Holy Spirit," I say.

"You shall be called," He had said.
Simon, I was.
I will renew you.
Peter, I became.

Day Four | Dwell on these Scriptures

Read Colossians 3:1-4:6 and Ephesians 5:15-16 through one time.

Reread Colossians 3 with the following in mind:

As you read, consider (you guessed it) the echoes of the creation story. This old creation has been put to death and a new creation raised in its place. Pay attention to verse 10, which echoes the phrasing of Genesis of being created in the image of the Creator God.

Consider this phrase "put on" used by Paul to contrast the actions of the old creation and the new. The Greek word used is *endyō* and means to "to sink into a garment."[16] God graciously provides garments for Adam and Eve when their sinful disobedience corrupted their image-bearer identity and purpose. But now, we put on garments that reflect our renewed identity and purpose as image-bearers, ones that truly reflect Christ Jesus and His commands.

As you read, notice the actions we are to put off sound similar to the 10 Commandments given Israel. God's standard for His creation has not changed. If anything, our understanding of it has expanded because of Jesus' example while He lived on earth.

Consider how this new creation is different from the corrupted version that we experience each day. It is to be renewed back to that original design where all of humanity is to partner with God in stewarding creation.

Consider the themes of promised hope, sacrificial love, shalom peace, and deeply-rooted joy that accompany living in alignment with Christ and His commands.

As you read, consider that just as Israel was instructed to live a set-apart life so others would know they were God's people, believers are encouraged to let their actions and their speech reflect the fact that they are followers of Christ's commands.

Reread Colossians 4:2-6 and Ephesians 5:15-16 with the following in mind:

In both Ephesians 5:16 and Colossians 4:5, the Greek word is *exagorazō* appears in reference to time.[17] This word is often translated as "redeem" and emphasizes the idea of purchasing something with a price in order to change its situation or condition. In these verses, there is a layer of opportunity and urgency, which is why some translations write it as "make the best use of the time."

As you read, consider how Christ followers are to act and speak according to His commands with wisdom, authority, and sacrifice—continually watching for opportunities to redeem, make right, the world around them. Paul even asks for prayer that God would bring such opportunities for him to share about Christ, pointing others towards this new creation living.

Consider how Paul instructs the Colossians to season their speech with salt, echoing the command to season the grain offering which symbolized thanksgiving and dedication of one's life to God.

Day Five | Dwell on this Theme

Ongoing Renewal
We are the Temple of the Holy Spirit. His presence does a work of renewal in and through our lives.

> Don't lie to each other, for you have stripped off your old sinful nature and all its wicked deeds. Put on your new nature, and be renewed as you learn to know your Creator and become like him. Colossians 3:9-10 (NLT)

A tour guide in Rome once explained to me that as archeologists dig down into the city, the layers of history meet them like the layers of a cake. They can see physically and figuratively how each historical period was built on the history of the years that preceded it.

In our current Church culture, we don't always do the hard work of excavating down through the layers on which our faith tradition rests. We take things at face-value, reading scripture through the lens of our reality instead of the ancient context it was written. And while the beauty of our faith still shines through, our understanding of it is shallow.

There are many threads that weave between the creation story, the exodus story, and our story. By noting them, phrases like "Jesus died for you", "you have the Holy Spirit", "let your light shine", "your identity is in Christ", and "live your life for Christ" suddenly have renewed meaning.

Just as God first focused on redeeming the Israelite's identity and purpose before leading them into the Promised Land, Jesus' death and resurrection redeems our identity and purpose as image-bearers on this side of the promised renewed creation.

God gave the Israelites commands to live by, setting them apart from the rest of the world, He does the same for us: love God and love others. And, as He gave specific instructions to Israel for rituals, feasts, and sacrifices, He does the same for the church with baptism, communion, and the great commission.

God redeemed Israel from the slave-identity and slave-purpose in Egypt, renaming them and consecrating them in the Wilderness. In the same way, we have been redeemed from our slave-identity and slave-purpose to the old creation corrupted by sinful disobedience (1 Cor 15:49) and given a renewed identity and purpose, one that is anchored in God's good design for humanity, in the figurative wilderness of this life.

Israel was freed from their Egyptian taskmasters then sanctified and consecrated for the task of being God's priestly representatives to the world. Through Christ's death and resurrection, we have been sanctified and consecrated for the task of being Christ's ambassadors, carrying His message of reconciliation (2 Cor 5:18-20). No longer are we working according to the will of that old identity. We are His representatives here on earth so others can be reconciled to God through Christ as well.

But, a single thread stands out from all the rest: God dwelling and co-ruling with His image-bearers.

When Jesus instituted Communion, He did so while observing the Passover Seder. When we remember Jesus as our savior with other believers, we do so rooted in a remembrance of God's enduring desire to dwell with humanity, to be their God and for them to be His people.

Jesus goes a step further and explains that the Spirit will dwell with them after He is gone. Then, He promises that God (both the Father and the Son) will come and make their home with those who love Jesus and follow His commands, echoing the promises God made to the Israelites.

> A single thread stands out from all the rest: God dwelling and co-ruling with His image-bearers.

This is why Paul, Peter, and other New Testament authors emphasized this idea that believers are the temple of the Holy Spirit (1 Corinthians 3:16, 1 Corinthians 6:19-20), anointed priests (Acts 1:7, 1 Peter 2:9, 1 John 2:20,27), and living sacrifices (Romans 12:1-8, Ephesians 5:1-2, 1 Peter 2:5). Just as Christ was all three in His life, death, and resurrection, we His renewed image-bearers, are as well.

Believers are both individually the dwelling place of God and collectively His temple. We refer to this collective temple as the Church. It is important to note that, unlike the Israelites, we have not been given a specific pattern for building this tabernacle/temple. We have a responsibility to care for the temple (hence why we have gifts of the Spirit), but we are not the one building it—God is. What a relief that while we partner with God in this ministry of reconciliation as messengers of the Gospel, it is ultimately up to God to draw people to Himself and redeem their lives. (1 Peter 2:5,9; 2 Cor 5:18-20)

While it's not up to us to save, we are called to live lives that point people clearly to Jesus through our words and actions. Everything we do is done as the temple of the Holy Spirit, as the priestly representative of Jesus, and as a living sacrifice.

Maybe you live out this concept really well. Or, maybe you are more like me. I don't always live with that at the forefront of my mind and constantly need the Spirit's help to do so.

Christ's death reconciled us to God. Christ's resurrection brought us new life. It is the renewing presence of the Spirit that serves as a sign of that redemptive work of Christ in our lives. A renewal that molds our life more into a life that reflects the image of Christ and one that God can use to renew the world around us.

> But thanks be to God, who gives us the victory through our Lord Jesus Christ. Therefore, my beloved brothers, be steadfast, immovable, always abounding in the work of the Lord, knowing that in the Lord your labor is not in vain. (1 Corinthians 15:57-58)

Day Six | Dwell on this Question

Do I live as if I believe I am a temple of God?

JOURNAL YOUR RESPONSES to the questions below:

What comes to mind when I think about God dwelling with me?

Do I treat my body and my life as a set-apart place where Heaven meets Earth? A living sacrifice?

Do I allow the Spirit to renew my life so that it looks more and more like Christ?

What areas of my life do I struggle to surrender to the Spirit for renewal?

Take a moment to write out your personal confession of God's renewing work in your life and through your life.

WEEK SIX
GOD DWELLS WITH US
IN THE NEW CREATION

WEEK FIVE | OVERVIEW

ADVENT SUNDAY/SABBATH

Dwell with God: in Anticipation

A NEW DAY

Dwell on this Truth: The purpose of a temple is to house the throne of God.

Advent Sunday | Dwell with God in Anticipation

PREPARE

Candle Set & Lighter
ALPHA OMEGA Ornament or Candle Label (if using)
Bible

Set aside distractions during this time of worship, reflection, and remembrance. Focus your thoughts on Christ's promise to return and dwell with us once more.

Begin by lighting the CHRIST CANDLE and reading John 1:1-5:

> In the beginning was the Word, and the Word was with God, and the Word was God. He was in the beginning with God. All things were made through him, and without Him was not anything made that was made. In him was life, and the life was the light of men. The light shines in the darkness, and the darkness has not overcome it.

REFLECT

As Christians, we experience hope, peace, joy, love, and renewal through the redemptive work of Christ and the Spirit dwelling with us. As you light the HOPE, PEACE, JOY, LOVE, and RENEWAL CANDLES reflect on the truth that while we experience these things, we still experience the heartache and pain of this broken world.

This should not surprise us, Jesus even warned that we would find ourselves going through challenging times but also reminded us that in Him, we find our *shalom* peace and deeply-rooted joy even in the midst of the devastation of the world.

This promise from Christ to return again is very layered and complex. We don't know all the details, though we do have prophecies from Israel's prophets, Jesus Himself, and many of the New Testament authors, specifically John.

What we do know is this: right now, each of our lives are new creations—mini Gardens of Eden—and together they form a larger new creation: the Church. But, one day, at the perfect time, there will be a total renewal of Heaven and Earth and at its center will be a New Jerusalem. It will be the dwelling place of God with His people. In that new creation, death, pain, and brokenness will no longer be a reality. All will be healed and made right.

While we don't know the day or the time, scripture encourages us to live as if it could happen today, allowing that sense of urgency to compel us to love others and to share the good news of God's salvation through Christ.

Go ahead and light the ANTICIPATION CANDLE (also called the Celebration Candle) as a reminder that Christ will come again and that we are in a season of waiting for this Second Advent.

We read scripture to be reminded of God's truth. In Romans 8:18-25, we are reminded that Jesus is coming again to make all things right. Read these verses:

Yet what we suffer now is nothing compared to the glory he will reveal to us later. For all creation is waiting eagerly for that future day when God will reveal who his children really are. Against its will, all creation was subjected to God's curse. But with eager hope, the creation looks forward to the day when it will join God's children in glorious freedom from death and decay. For we know that all creation has been groaning as in the pains of childbirth right up to the present time.

And we believers also groan, even though we have the Holy Spirit within us as a foretaste of future glory, for we long for our bodies to be released from sin and suffering. We, too, wait with eager hope for the day when God will give us our full rights as his adopted children, including the new bodies he has promised us. We were given this hope when we were saved. (If we already have something, we don't need to hope for it. But if we look forward to something we don't yet have, we must wait patiently and confidently.) (NLT)

REJOICE

At this time place your ANTICIPATION ornament or candle label. This ornament has two Greek letters on it: Alpha and Omega. In Revelation, Jesus tells John that He is the Alpha and the Omega. Those are the first and last letters of the Greek alphabet. This ornament reminds us that Jesus has dwelled with us since the beginning and He will continue to dwell with us for eternity.

Before you end this time of reflection and rejoicing, take a moment to dwell on this question:

How can I better live as if Jesus is returning tomorrow?

Take a moment to give thanks:

> Father God, thank You for Your desire to dwell with us. Even when humanity chose sinful disobedience, throughout the generations, You have forgiven and made a way for Your people to dwell with You. We ANTICIPATE the day when your original design for dwelling with us is restored. Amen.

This Advent season, we have remembered the First Advent, the first coming of Jesus as the Messiah. Today, we remember that there will be a Second Advent when Jesus returns to make all things new and right. As you close this time of reflection and rejoicing, add your voice with those generations before and pray:

Come, Lord Jesus, come.

A New Day I Dwell on this Truth

The purpose of a temple is to house the throne of God.

IMAGE-BEARER: A NEW EVE

I fall through the page into the space bent between time before and time eternal. Hovering in what is not known while waiting to find out what is, I find myself wondering if I should be afraid? There is no sickening feeling in my stomach—my usual signal to be on alert. But, it's not there. In fact, a settledness has taken root deep in my bones and spread out to my nerves.

That settledness vibrates the space around me with its energy. At first, I think it is radiating out from deep within my bones but, I quickly realize, that's not correct. The settledness is so great around me, it has permeated my being and cultivated little offshoots mirroring its presence within my body.

The space flexes and then contorts itself into a structured form right before me.

And around me.
And in me.

I am suddenly deeply aware that I have been invited into a sacred moment. I am not afraid, but I feel unworthy to be here. This structure is awe inspiring in its expanse and its depth but before I can admire its fullness, I am thrust forward.

Deeper.
Farther.
Further.
Invited.

The energy that carries me deposits me with care on the ground before a large and looming tree. It is centered in what I immediately want to call a jungle because of the sheer thickness of the vegetation around me, but I notice the cultivated edge, the trimmed leaves, the pruned branches, the cut away pasture, and identify it, instead, as a garden. The colors of the plants, flowers, and tree leaves are so vibrant, they dance on the lines of my vision. And their smell? Each individual scent swirls with its neighbor's to create an aroma that tickles my nose with delight before mingling with the inhaled breath it rides into my lungs. I feel a pleasant sensation warm my chest. It reminds me of the settledness that is still rooted deep in my bones.

I feel a warm, padded thing walk over the top of my foot and I immediately jump at the shock of the sensation. In turn, my quick movement startles the animal, a small snowy-white bunny, and it darts away from me. My eyes follow it as it scampers over a large and protruding root of the tree. I take a moment to study the looming champion and realize that the light engulfs the tree around and within, much like how the settledness radiated around and within me. The light emanates and permeates from both within and without, weaving in and out around its branches, coming from within the very branches itself and yet not contained to it.

"Am I about to die?" I ask out loud. Though, I'm not sure why since I am alone.

Except, I'm not.

I feel the life of His presence pulsating out from the tree and towards me like blood through veins with the beat of a heart.

The tree is consumed by His presence and yet not burned.

The way I feel right now, I realize.

I drop to my knees, aware that any other action would be an inappropriate response to the holy ground on which I stand.

Look up.

The command comes from within and around and before me.

I obey, pushing myself up from the ground and sitting back on my heels. The pulse of divinity continues in a steady and faithful rhythm but the light shifts from the tree and casts a shadow on the ground beside it. The shadow grows, its form shifting as well from a defined trunk with branches to the stem of a lampstand with seven branches that end in cups. I recognize it as the temple's lampstand. It grows larger and larger until the shadow rises from the ground and stands before the tree, both a shield and a veil.

A shadow might not be the best word to describe it, as shadows often bring to mind darkness. This shape was not one of darkness, in fact it held within its design hope and joy. But it doesn't, cannot, compare to the life-giving tree behind it.

I raise a hand to touch the shadow but as I reach out, the light from the tree burns into the shadow and disintegrates it into little pieces. They flutter to the ground like ash and collect in a pile at my toes.

The edges of the shadow remain, but in its center the shadow has been consumed by the light.

North to south.
East to west.
A cross to cover all of life.

The light bursts forth from the cross shape and I instinctively shield my eyes with my arm. But, the rhythmic pulse of His presence guides my arm away from my face. With my vision unblocked, I can see the light that burst forth has pulled back into itself and gathered into a swirl. It picks up speed with each completed cycle.

Swirling.
Swirling.
Rushing.
Rushing.

The sight and sound merge and I hear the violent wind before and around and within me.

The swirl breaks out into a million little pieces of light, flinging every which way, many of which I can no longer see. I am aware of their presence, just like I am still aware of His presence.

I feel a warmth above me and lift my eyes to see one of the lights hovering. I am not sure if it has taken on the shape of a flame or if my eyes and my brain are attempting to make sense of it with something I understand.

Whereas I could feel the pulse of His presence emitting from the tree before me, now I can feel it radiating from within me.

Just like that settledness in my bones.

I feel compelled to look down at the palms of my hands. I expect to see them empty. But instead a box with a bow sits right there in the middle of my right hand. I pinch the ribbon of the bow with my left and tug. The ribbon slips off and the sides of the box fall away in unison.

What remains is a crackling ball of energy that I am simultaneously in awe of and terrified by. I hesitate, unsure I want to do what is necessary.

But, I know.

I know that I am known and this gift is created specifically for me and to be used by me. With a decisive move, I scoop it up and press it against my heart. Where I expected shocks of electricity to be endured, I instead feel a tingle that hits every nerve from head to toe.

It is like my system has been recalibrated and I can actually feel for the first time in my life.

And what I feel is awe.

Awe as understanding floods the unused spaces of my mind and I comprehend the layered complexity of the images I just watched take their turn before me.

The Tree.
The Lamp.
The Cross.
The People.

All pointing to *the light*, that life-giving presence that envelopes and does not consume. The one that rises in victory over darkness.

Awe is what I feel.
Worship is what I do.

I alternate between pressing my face to the ground and scrambling to my feet to dance without reserve. I am not sure which is the more proper response to standing at the foot of the Throne of Grace and in the presence of the Almighty.

It is during my fourth period of dancing that I notice the others, those parts of the light that had dispersed, gathering from the corners and distances.

Called back to their home.
Back to their dwelling place.

Back and, yet, forward.

Because this is not the original Garden.
It is a new thing.

A fuller expression of His creativity.

Filled with abundance.
Filled to the ends with His glory.

Shalom. True and complete.

There is no lamp, no sun, because *the light* sits on the throne at the center of this cosmic tabernacle. It is all and everything. Heaven and Earth, Garden and City.

With a clear and strong voice the one seated on the throne proclaims, "It is done."

I close my eyes as I feel the words within me and around me and before me.

Radiating out and permeating within.
Enveloping but not consuming.
Loving and Healing.

My eyes open to the ceiling of my bedroom. I am no longer in that beautiful garden but am on the floor next to my bed. It takes me a second to register that my head hurts. "Ow!" A quick glance around reveals that I hit my head on the end table when I fell.

My roommate rolls over in her bed, flips on the lamp on her end table, and flaps her hand to get my attention.

You okay? She signs with one hand while covering a yawn with the other.

I rub the side of my head. *Just sat up too fast and hit my head.* I sign my answer.

She mumbles, "okay," forgetting to sign it, then rolls back over, pulling the blanket back over her shoulders.

Situated back under my own covers, my mind drifts back to the image of the New Creation and with it comes the feeling of awe and the desire to worship. I know I won't be able to explain what I saw to anyone, especially not my roommate, but that feels okay. Like this image has been given to me as a gift. Not for any grand revelation but simply as a reminder that I am known, loved, and chosen.

Intentionally designed to dwell with my Creator.

I tug my covers up around my chin and smile before falling back into a peace-filled sleep.

The Second Advent

Revelation 22:12-17, 20 (NLT, emphasis added) "Look, I Jesus am coming soon, bringing my reward with me to repay all people according to their deeds. I am the Alpha and the Omega, the First and the Last, the Beginning and the End."

Blessed are those who wash their robes. They will be permitted to enter through the gates of the city and eat the fruit from the tree of life. Outside the city are the dogs—the sorcerers, the sexually immoral, the murderers, the idol worshipers, and all who love to live a lie.

"I, Jesus, have sent my angel to give you this message for the churches. I am both the source of David and the heir to his throne. I am the bright morning star."

The Spirit and the bride say, **"Come."**

Let anyone who hears this say, **"Come."**

Let anyone who is thirsty come.
Let anyone who desires drink freely from the water of life.

He who is the faithful witness to all these things says,

"Yes, I am coming soon!"

Amen! Come, Lord Jesus!

NOTES

1. You can learn more about our family's journey in practicing a weekly, 24-hour Sabbath at *simplysabbath.com*

2. Jefferson Bethke, *To Hell with the Hustle* (Thomas Nelson, 2019).

3. In Leviticus 25, the Israelites are commanded to observe a sabbatical every seven years. Land was to lie fallow and debts were to be forgiven. After seven cycles, the 50th year was the Year of Jubilee, during which debts were to be forgiven, slaves set free, and land reverted to its original owner.

4. While wording for these definitions are my own, I referenced both Merriam-Webster.com and Dictionary.com as I wrote them.

5. Bible Project, *Sabbath Study Notes* (Bible Project, 2020), accessed Nov 7, 2023. https://bibleproject.com/view-resource/336/

6. The *Sabbath Study Notes* Bible Project compiled goes deep into the topic of Sabbath, rest, and the seventh day. The Bible Project also recorded an in-depth podcast discussion and created an animated video exploring this topic. https://bibleproject.com/explore/video/sabbath-video/

7. "redeem." *Merriam-Webster.com*. 2023. Accessed Nov 7, 2023. https://www.merriam-webster.com/

8. William D. Mounce, editor, *Mounce's Complete Expository Dictionary of Old & New Testament Words* (Zondervan, 2006), "Redeem, Redemption," accessed Nov 7, 2023 via https://biblegateway.com

9. Mounce's Complete Expository Dictionary also explains that if no one was able to redeem the land or an enslaved family member, the land would revert to its original owner in the year of Jubilee. This is an interesting concept to explore further considering Jesus started His ministry reading from Isaiah 61.

10. "G1722 - en - Strong's Greek Lexicon (kjv)." Blue Letter Bible. Web. Accessed Nov 8, 2023. https://www.blueletterbible.org/lexicon/g1722/kjv/tr/0-1

11. The Bible Project created a videos exploring the word "gospel." You can view it at: https://bibleproject.com/explore/video/euangelion-gospel/

12. Edward W. Goodrick. *NIV Exhaustive Concordance Dictionary*, (Zondervan, 2015), accessed via biblegateway.com on Nov 8, 2023.

13. Edward W. Goodrick. *NIV Exhaustive Concordance Dictionary*, (Zondervan, 2015), accessed via biblegateway.com on Nov 8, 2023.

14. "G4161 - poiēma - Strong's Greek Lexicon (kjv)." Blue Letter Bible. Accessed Nov 8, 2023. https://www.blueletterbible.org/lexicon/g4161/kjv/tr/0-1/

15. Word Wool Team, "History of Poetry," wordwool.com, accessed Nov 8, 2023. https://wordwool.com/history-of-poetry/

16. "G1746 - endyō - Strong's Greek Lexicon (kjv)." Blue Letter Bible. Accessed Nov 8, 2023. https://www.blueletterbible.org/lexicon/g1746/kjv/tr/0-1/

17. "G1805 - exagorazō - Strong's Greek Lexicon (kjv)." Blue Letter Bible. Accessed Nov 8, 2023. https://www.blueletterbible.org/lexicon/g1805/kjv/tr/0-1/

ABOUT THE AUTHOR

RACHEL FAHRENBACH creates novel ways to approach scripture study, literally. By combining her skill for creative writing with her bent for coaching, Rachel utilizes various mediums (such as books, podcasts, and social media) to lead readers through fictional stories to the most important (and absolutely truest) story of all: God's love for humanity. Originally from Chicago, Rachel now resides in Alabama with her husband and three kiddos.

MORE FROM RACHEL

Rest & Reflect: A 12-Week Guided Journal Designed to help you intentionally rest each week with Jesus while diving into questions about identity, purpose, and belonging. Purchase your copy on Amazon.

RachelFahrenbach.com Book updates, resources, and more!

SimplySabbath.com Find resources (downloads, podcast episodes, etc.) to help you implement a simple, family Sabbath into your week.

TheBusinessofChristianFiction.com A podcast exploring what it takes to get your novel into the hands of a reader.

Facebook and Instagram @rachelfahrenbach

Made in the USA
Las Vegas, NV
01 December 2023